What Can I Make With This ...

Frickin'
Chicken?!

Pamela Gelsomini

Published in the United States of America
by Dish off the Block

ISBN 978-1-7358103-1-7 (hardcover)
ISBN 978-1-7358103-0-0 (paperback)

Contents

Dedication

The smell of leg of lamb in the oven... Thanksgiving turkey busting with stuffing... heavenly sighs when biting into a big spoonful of chicken fricassee over mashed potatoes... memories of baking Christmas cookies... a freezer stocked each summer with enough stuffed zucchinis to last for years...

Food, for me, is about love and sharing that love with family and friends. My grandmother, Alice Andrews, whom I lovingly named 'Becky' at a very young age, was not a fancy cook, but she was an excellent cook making hearty, delicious New England fare that brought family and friends around the table together. Anytime you walked into her house the aromas embraced you and you felt an overwhelming sense of family, togetherness, and love.

Her memory, her cooking, and her unwavering love and support have served as inspiration to me over and over again as I grew up, went through school, started a business, and now on my new journey as a food blogger and cookbook author.

So, Becky, I dedicate my first cookbook to you. I wish you were still here as I know you would be so proud of this moment, but I know you are looking down and want you to know what an impact you had in making me who I am today and why I am so passionate about food and its ability to show and spread love.

Acknowledgments

A lot of special people in my life have made Dish off the Block and this cookbook possible. I would like to say thank you to a few.

The Dish off the Block Team

It all started with meeting a couple of my high school girlfriends for lunch. I had recently sold my shoe insole business and 'retired' from that journey after an amazing 20 years traveling the globe for the footwear business.

"What should I do next?" I asked. "Something with food?" I have always been a passionate cook and foodie. For many years, I wanted to write a cookbook to memorialize my recipes and thought, this might be the time.

My girlfriends, Tracy Coyne and Stephanie Neil, who have their own PR business, said, "Wait... you will need a following first. Why not start a food blog?" And so, we did. Dish off the Block was born. Tracy, Steph, and I are now partners in crime constantly noodling ways to build our brand and the DotB business. Their wisdom, hard work, and passion for our vision is the very reason we have come this far. Thank you, ladies. Oh, the places we will go!!

My Family

The Garbage Disposal—My son, Andrew, is probably the biggest fan of my cooking. Always curious and willing to try anything I put in front of him, usually offering rave reviews. His contribution to this business is significant, for without his massive appetite (20 year-old young man) and love of leftovers, I would never have been able to cook the quantities of food that allowed me to build a repertoire of recipes, numbering in the hundreds.

The Food Critic—My daughter, Laura (16), is a purist when it comes to food. She too, due to strict training as a young child and the one-bite rule in our house, will try anything I make, BUT she's my mac & cheese girl all day long. When I say I am making pizza, she retorts—"for the love of God, can you just make a plain cheese pizza??" She doesn't normally get her request granted as I thoroughly enjoy the challenge of making something new and winning over the toughest critic in the house... and I usually do.

The Dishwasher—My husband, Nick, has tirelessly and patiently cleaned up a kitchen that, most days, resembles the aftereffects of a tornado passing through. Ten million thank-yous (one for each cleaned dish) are not enough to my forever guy for the endless love and support... except when I make something too spicy for his tender palate!

To all of my family and friends who gather around the table to enjoy the food I truly love to make: Thank you!

Foreword

My niece Pam, a gifted visual artist and entrepreneur, has always been fascinated with food as an expression of her multifaceted boundless creativity. My first experience with her fervor began when, as a 10 year old, she would visit her beloved Grammy "Becky" in the summertime and stockpile the freezer with her zucchini creations.

Since then, Pam has pursued her culinary abilities in the direction of both savory comfort and world class gourmet. One of her signature dishes, my regular soul-nourishing request, has always been chicken pot pie. Throughout the years she has refined my palate with preparations of every cuisine imaginable full of love, invention, and the most delectable combination of flavors. Each meal, an original work of art, speaks to her passion and seriousness as an epicurean.

Cooking is not a natural talent I possess. Whenever I've been asked to put together a special occasion appetizer or entrée, Pam has rescued me with step-by-step simplicity resulting in rave reviews and repeated requests. That's what you will discover in these pages—heightened homestyle chicken recipes and more sophisticated dishes your family and guests will crave ever after. As my family and I know from decades spent in her kitchen, Pam's hallmark word for taste test approval is a simple "yummy" and What Can I Make With This Frickin' Chicken is simply that.

WITH LOVE AND PRIDE,

AUNT MARY

Introduction

Every day in households across America someone is asking the question: "What's for dinner?" And, the answer—on at least one or more days during the week—is, "Chicken." Of course, there's always that pesky follow-up question of, "What kind of chicken?" To which the typical response is a resounding "I don't know!" And, once dinner is served it will usually be one of a handful of go-to chicken dishes, such as baked chicken, fried chicken, chicken parmesan, chicken stir fry or even the ever popular chicken nuggets.

It's boring and quite frankly exhausting to get stuck in a chicken recipe rut.

Personally, I don't have this problem as I have an over-active appetite for creativity in the kitchen. For the past few decades I have been inventing recipes that combine a variety of flavors and techniques that have resulted in unique culinary concepts from everyday ingredients. I have entered—and won—many recipe contests online and on the road as I often travel to participate in food sport competitions, such as the Gilroy Garlic Festival, the Cornbread Festival, and the World Food Championships.

With these kinds of experiences, I'm often the person my friends and family turn to when they need a little inspiration in the kitchen. Like my sister-in-law Lisa, who, at least once a week calls me asking for ideas. In her house, with three growing boys, chicken has always been a popular protein. But the boys are hard to impress week after week. When she calls, I can always picture her on the other end of the phone, her hands on her hips as she stares down at the raw chicken on her counter, her voice imploring me to help as she exclaims, "What can I make with this frickin' chicken?"

Each time I would help her concoct a new chicken concept that her family would devour. (And they did!) And, it made me think, if my friends and family are having this problem, so are millions of other home cooks. And, voila! This cookbook was conceived!

In the pages that follow, you will find a variety of chicken recipes I've developed over the years. They are designed to be easy and yet taste and look sophisticated on the plate. They are guaranteed to wow your family and give you a lot of credibility in the kitchen. Most of all, preparing food should be fun, not stressful, and that's what I hope these recipes provide for you. Experiment a little, get out of your comfort zone and make something that may seem difficult—but really isn't, I promise! I've designed my recipes to be achievable for the everyday cook. There is a place for you at the bottom of each recipe page to "rate the dish" so that you can always go back to your favorite four star picks!

I have been blogging and making videos about recipe development for quite some time now, but I do hope you enjoy my first foray into the cookbook category. If you don't, well, no harm, no "fowl," but I think you will!

Keep on cookin'!

13

APPETIZERS

Appetizers

sesame chicken bites
with spicy dip

2 tablespoons rice wine vinegar
2 tablespoons sesame oil
1 tablespoon garlic, chopped
2 tablespoons soy sauce
2 boneless chicken breasts
    (about 1 ½ pounds)

¼ cup white sesame seeds
¼ cup black sesame seeds
¾ cup corn starch
Peanut oil for frying
48 fresh snow peas (strings
    removed)

THE SPICY DIP:

1 tablespoon rice wine vinegar
2 tablespoons Thai chili sauce
1 tablespoon soy sauce
1 teaspoon sesame oil

2 teaspoons fresh ginger root,
    minced
¾ cup Hellmann's light mayonnaise
1 tablespoon brown sugar

In a medium bowl combine the vinegar, sesame oil, garlic, and soy sauce to create a marinade. Cut chicken into bite size chunks and add to the marinade. Cover and refrigerate overnight.

Mix sesame seeds, corn starch, and flour in a pie plate or shallow baking dish. Heat ¼-inch of peanut oil in a large frying pan over medium heat. Dip marinated chicken pieces in the sesame mixture to coat. Place in hot oil and cook in small batches until lightly browned on all sides. Remove from pan and drain on paper towels.

Steam snow peas in boiling salted water for 1-2 minutes until bright green, but still crisp. Drain in a colander and rinse with cold water to stop cooking. Wrap one snow pea around each piece of chicken and fasten with a toothpick.

Mix all dip ingredients together in a small bowl and whisk until smooth.

Serve warm or at room temperature on a platter with dip in the center.

Rate It!
☆☆☆☆☆

rosemary, parmesan and cracked black pepper panko wings

¾ cup grated parmesan cheese (plus 1 tablespoon for garnish)
¾ cup panko bread crumbs
¼ cup rosemary leaves, stemmed and chopped
2 teaspoons fresh ground black pepper
1 teaspoon salt
½ cup Hellmann's Light mayonnaise
3 pounds chicken wings, tips removed, flats and drumettes separated
2-3 tablespoons olive oil

Preheat oven to 400 degrees.

Combine the parmesan, panko, rosemary, black pepper, and salt in a pie plate or shallow baking dish.

Using a pastry brush, coat each piece of chicken on both sides with the Hellmann's mayo, then press into the parmesan panko mixture to coat. Place the wings on a baking sheet topped with foil and sprayed with non-stick cooking spray. Do not crowd the wings.

Drizzle the olive oil over the tops of the wings on the baking sheet. Bake for 30-35 minutes until golden and juices run clear when pierced with a knife.

Garnish with parmesan and rosemary sprigs.

This recipe is delicious on wings as the perfect game day snack, but it's also fantastic on larger cuts of chicken like thighs or breasts for an easy sheet pan dinner.

Rate It!
☆☆☆☆☆

addiction chicken lettuce wraps

THE SAUCE:

¼ cup rice wine vinegar
¼ cup oyster sauce
1 ½ tablespoons soy sauce
1 teaspoon sriracha sauce
1 teaspoon sesame oil
1 teaspoon brown sugar
2 teaspoons corn starch

2 tablespoons peanut oil
1 cup mushrooms, minced
6 cloves garlic, minced
1 tablespoon fresh ginger root, minced
1 jalapeno, minced
1 pound ground chicken

1 teaspoon **Dish off the Block Ragin' Cajun Spice Blend**
1 cup red bell pepper, finely chopped
1, 8-ounce can chopped water chestnuts, drained
¾ cup scallions, chopped white and green parts
1 teaspoon tuxedo sesame seeds (black and white mixed)

1 large head butter or Boston lettuce
2 cups bean sprouts
Optional: Chopped honey roasted peanuts

Combine all of the sauce ingredients in a small bowl and whisk until the corn starch dissolves. Set aside.

Heat 1 tablespoon peanut oil in a large deep skillet or wok over medium high heat. Add the mushrooms, garlic, ginger, and jalapeno to the pan and cook for 3 minutes, stirring frequently, until fragrant and the juice released from the mushrooms has mostly cooked off.

Add the ground chicken, Cajun seasoning, red bell pepper, and water chestnuts to the pan. Continue to cook, breaking up the chicken with a spatula for 3-4 minutes until the chicken is cooked through. Add the sauce and ½ cup of the scallions to the pan, continuing to cook for 2 more minutes, stirring as the sauce thickens.

Serve the hot chicken mixture, garnished with sesame seeds in a serving bowl with lettuce leaves and bean sprouts on the side. To assemble the lettuce wraps, place about ¼ cup of the chicken mixture on a lettuce leaf, top with bean sprouts, peanuts, and fold together like a taco!!

Rate It!
☆☆☆☆☆

mini chicken and black bean empanada bites

These yummy bites come together quickly and use one of my favorite shortcut products—frozen puff pastry dough. Found in the freezer section of most major grocery stores, your guests will never know that you didn't make it yourself. You can also make these treats in advance and freeze until you are ready to serve them.

THE FILLING:

1 cup chicken breast, cooked and chopped into small pieces
1 cup black beans, rinsed
1, 4-ounce can chopped green chilies
½ cup red bell pepper, diced
¼ cup green bell pepper, diced
¼ cup frozen corn kernels, thawed
4 ounces cream cheese, softened
¾ cup pepper jack cheese, shredded
½ teaspoon salt
½ teaspoon cumin

1, 17.3-ounce package frozen puff pastry dough, thawed (2 sheets)
2 eggs, beaten
1 cup salsa or pico de gallo

Preheat oven to 400 degrees.

Combine all of the filling ingredients in a large bowl and mix to fully combine.

Unfold the puff pastry sheets and roll each on a lightly floured surface to 9x14-inch rectangles. Using a 3-inch round pastry cutter, cut 12 circles out of each piece of dough. Roll any scraps and cut 2 additional rounds.

Place a heaping tablespoon of the filling in the center of each circle. Brush beaten egg around the edge on one half of each round. Gently stretch one side of the dough over the filling and seal on the other side creating 'half-moon' shapes. Crimp the edges with a fork to seal.

Place on foil lined baking sheets sprayed with non-stick cooking spray. Brush the tops of each empanada with the egg wash. Bake for 25-35 minutes until puffed and golden brown. Serve with salsa on the side for dipping.

Rate It!
☆☆☆☆

chicken parmesan meatballs

THE MEATBALLS:

1 pound ground chicken
1 egg, beaten
¼ teaspoon black pepper
½ teaspoon salt
2 teaspoons **Dish off the Block
   Ciao Bella Italian Spice Blend**

½ cup grated parmesan cheese
½ cup Italian breadcrumbs
⅓ cup flat leaf parsley, chopped
15, ½-inch cubes provolone cheese

THE BREADING:

1 egg
⅓ cup parmesan cheese
½ cup panko breadcrumbs

⅓ cup olive oil
1 cup spaghetti or marinara sauce
Parmesan and parsley for garnish

Combine all of the meatball ingredients, except provolone, in a large bowl. Mix with your hands until everything is well incorporated. Roll into meatballs about the size of golf balls (about 15). Press one cube of provolone into each meatball and form the meat around the cheese to completely seal. Roll in your hands to make perfect balls. Place on a parchment lined cookie sheet and place in the freezer for 30 minutes. This will help them maintain their shape when frying.

Create a breading station. Place the egg in a shallow dish. Combine the parmesan and panko in another dish.

Preheat oven to 350 degrees.

Heat the oil over medium heat. Dip each meatball in the egg to coat and then roll in the panko-parmesan mixture. Fry in hot oil until golden brown on all sides. Place back on the parchment lined cookie sheet and place in the oven for 15-20 minutes to completely cook through. Cheese will be gooey and stringy on the inside. Serve with warm marinara on the side for dipping if you are serving as an appetizer. Also, delicious over pasta for dinner! Mangia!!

This recipe was inspired by the traditional Italian dish Chicken Parmigiana. Visit the blog and watch the video to get a recipe just like your Nonna used to make!

Rate It!
☆☆☆☆☆

finger lickin'... oh that chicken, spicy, sweet... can't wait to eat... sticky, crunchy... they're the best... there's no doubt these beat the rest... wings!

THE GLAZE:

1, 18-ounce jar apricot preserves
1 jalapeno, chopped fine
3 large garlic cloves, peeled and
    chopped fine
1 inch fresh ginger root chopped fine
2 tablespoons sriracha sauce
1 tablespoon soy sauce
1 tablespoon fish sauce
1 ½ cups brown sugar packed

5 pounds chicken wings, tips removed, flats and drumettes separated
2 teaspoons salt
2 teaspoons black pepper
4-5 cups vegetable oil (for frying)
2 scallions, chopped for garnish
blue cheese or ranch dressing for dipping

THE COATING:

1 cup flour
1 teaspoon baking powder
1 cup corn starch
½ cup vodka
1 ½-2 cups water

To make the glaze, combine the apricot preserves, jalapeno, garlic, ginger, sriracha, soy, fish sauce, and brown sugar in a large saucepan. Bring to a low boil and whisk to combine until preserves melt and glaze is smooth. Reduce heat to low and continue cooking, stirring occasionally, for about 10 minutes until the sauce becomes syrupy. The glaze may bubble up during this process. Continue whisking when this happens so the sauce doesn't boil over.

While the glaze cooks, mix the flour, baking powder, and corn starch in a medium bowl. Whisking constantly, gradually add vodka and 1 ½-2 cups water. The batter should be the consistency of a thin pancake batter.

Season the chicken wings generously with the salt and pepper on both sides.

Heat vegetable oil in a deep fryer (or large Dutch oven) to 350 degrees. Working in batches and returning oil to 350 degrees between batches, coat chicken in batter, letting excess drip back into bowl, and fry until skin is golden and chicken is crisp and cooked through, about 8-10 minutes, depending on size. When placing the wings in the hot oil, hold the end and dip in the oil for about 5-7 seconds before letting go. This will keep them from sticking to the bottom of the fryer/pan.

Transfer to a wire rack set inside a baking sheet to drain. Using tongs, dip hot wings in the warm glaze, turn to coat, then transfer wings back to the wire rack. Cool for 5 minutes allowing excess glaze to drip off and transfer to a platter. Serve wings garnished with chopped scallions and blue cheese (or ranch) dressing on the side for dipping.

Rate It!

☆☆☆☆

These sticky-spicy-sweet wings have won multiple competitions including the World Food Championships Super Qualifier in 2019!

chicken satay skewers
with thai peanut sauce

This recipe and so many others are inspired by my many trips to Southeast Asia and the incredible flavors I experienced during my travels to China, Vietnam, Indonesia, Thailand, and Korea.

THE MARINADE:

⅓ cup smooth peanut butter
¼ cup rice wine vinegar
¼ cup soy sauce
1 tablespoon sriracha sauce
2 tablespoons brown sugar

1 tablespoon honey
1 tablespoon chopped garlic
3 tablespoons orange juice
1 teaspoon sesame oil

1 ½-2 pounds chicken tenders
1 tablespoon sesame seeds
2 scallions, chopped

Whisk all of the marinade ingredients together in a medium bowl until smooth. Add the chicken tenders and toss to fully coat. Let marinate for at least 3 hours or overnight. At the same time submerge your wooden skewers in water (a 9x13-inch baking dish works well for this) and let soak until ready to cook.

Bring the marinated chicken to room temperature 30 minutes before cooking. Thread one skewer through each tender lengthwise and place on a plate or baking sheet (just to transfer easily to the grill). Reserve any excess marinade for sauce.

Set grill to medium high and let it reach about 400-450 degrees before adding the chicken skewers. Cook the chicken about 2-3 minutes on the first side and then flip each and cook another 2-3 minutes until just cooked through on the other side. This will vary slightly depending on the size of the tenders, but does not take long.

Place any remaining marinade in a small sauce pan and bring to a low boil. Cook for 5 minutes stirring constantly to cook out the raw chicken juices and reduce the sauce. Brush the chicken skewers on both sides with the sauce and garnish with sesame seeds and scallions.

Great as an appetizer or full meal over rice. This marinade can also be used for full boneless breasts or chicken thighs as well!

Rate It!
☆☆☆☆☆

mini chicken cordon bleu puffs

1, 17.3 ounce package puff pastry
    sheets (2 sheets), thawed
4 tablespoons grainy mustard
4 tablespoons honey
2 cups cooked chicken breast,
    chopped into small pieces

1 cup ham steak, cut into ½-inch dice
2 ½ cups Jarlsberg or Swiss cheese,
    shredded
1 teaspoon salt
1 teaspoon black pepper
1 egg, beaten

Preheat oven to 400 degrees.

Lightly flour your counter and unfold the thawed puff pastry sheets. Roll each into 12x14-inch rectangle.

Combine the mustard and 2 tablespoons of the honey in a small bowl. Spread this mixture evenly over the 2 sheets, all the way to the edges, leaving 1 inch on either end of the 12-inch side exposed. Spread the chicken over the dough, followed by the ham, and two cups of the cheese. Season evenly with the salt and pepper.

Starting with the 12-inch side that is not exposed, roll the dough, jelly-roll style, pushing any ingredients that fall out of edges back inside. Brush the exposed edge with egg and seal the roll tightly.

Using a serrated knife, cut the roll into 12, 1-inch rounds taking care not to crush when cutting. Place each roll, cut side up, on a foil lined baking sheet that has been sprayed with non-stick cooking spray. Brush each round on the exposed sides and top with the egg wash. Sprinkle with remaining cheese and drizzle with the remaining honey.

Bake for 20-30 minutes until puffed and golden brown.

Rate It!

☆☆☆☆☆

grilled thai chicken lettuce wraps
with sweet pickled cukes and three sauces

THE MARINADE (AND SAUCE):

⅔ cup peanut butter
4 tablespoons rice wine vinegar
4 tablespoons soy sauce
2 tablespoons brown sugar, packed
2 teaspoons sriracha sauce
2 teaspoons sesame oil
2 tablespoons fresh ginger root, peeled and finely
    minced
4 teaspoons garlic cloves, peeled and minced
1 pound chicken tenders (or chicken breast cut into
    thin strips)
¼ cup honey roasted peanuts, chopped

THE SWEET PICKLED CUCUMBERS:

⅓ cup rice wine vinegar
¼ cup water
¼ cup sugar
2 teaspoons black sesame seeds
¼ teaspoon salt
2 cups English cucumber, peeled and chopped

Red cabbage leaf "bowls" are pretty for serving.

THE SESAME RICE NOODLES:

1 ½ cups vermicelli rice noodles
1 teaspoon sesame oil
¼ teaspoon salt

THE WRAPS:

2 heads Boston butter lettuce
2 cups carrots, julienned or spiralized
2 cups bean sprouts
½ cup cilantro leaves

THE HOISIN HONEY SAUCE:

2 tablespoons hoisin sauce
1 tablespoon honey
1 tablespoon rice wine vinegar
1 tablespoon water
1 tablespoon scallions, chopped

THE OTHER SAUCES:

⅓ cup Thai chili sauce
⅓ cup sriracha mayonnaise

Combine all of the marinade ingredients in a small bowl and whisk until smooth. Place chicken tenders in a large Ziploc™ bag and add ½ cup of the marinade in the bag and massage to coat. Refrigerate for at least 2 hours or, preferably, overnight.

Make your marinated cucumbers at least 30 minutes before you are ready to serve the wraps. Combine the vinegar, water, sugar, sesame seeds, and salt in a large jar. Shake to combine. Add the chopped cucumbers and shake again. Set aside and let the marinade do its magic.

Cover the vermicelli rice noodles with hot water and let sit for 20-30 minutes until soft. Drain and toss with the sesame oil and salt. Set aside.

Heat your grill to medium high (about 400 degrees) or heat a lightly oiled grill pan on your stove top. Place the marinated chicken on the grill and cook about 1-2 minutes per side, depending on the thickness, until just cooked through. Remove to a plate and sprinkle with chopped nuts. Set aside until ready to serve. These can be served warm or room temperature.

Prepare the hoisin honey sauce by simply whisking all of the ingredients together until smooth.

Rate It!

☆☆☆☆☆

For the peanut sauce, combine ⅓ cup of the remaining marinade (that has not touched the raw chicken) with 2 tablespoons water and whisk until smooth.

Place each of these sauces along with the store-bought Thai chili sauce and sriracha mayo in small bowls for serving. Create a serving plate with lettuce leaves on one side and all of the other ingredients around them. To eat, take one lettuce leaf and layer the remaining ingredients on top with desired sauce. Wrap and eat taco-style! Sooo good!

Note—shrimp also works really well as a substitute or in addition to the chicken!

SOUPS AND CHOWDERS

Contents

classic chicken soup
like your mama used to make

Classic chicken soup starts with a basic stock consisting of chicken bones and a 'mirepoix' which is a combination of onions, celery, and carrots. This is a blank canvas that makes a rich stock that can then be enhanced with other flavors and textures from your pantry like spices, rice, beans, and pasta or added vegetables like spinach, kale, corn, and so much more.

1, 4-5 pound fresh chicken or chicken parts (or one chicken carcass with meat left on the bone)
1 tablespoon salt
1 tablespoon black pepper
2 tablespoons olive oil
2 large onions, chopped
1 bunch celery, chopped into ¾-inch pieces (about 4-5 cups)

2 quarts chicken stock
3 large soft chicken bouillon cubes (or 2 tablespoons chicken base)
1, 2 pound bag carrots, peeled and cut into 1-inch thick rounds
¼ cup fresh parsley, chopped

OPTIONAL:

1-2 cans cannellini beans, drained
2-3 cups baby kale or spinach
1 ½ cups fresh tortellini

2 cups egg noodles, cooked al dente
½ cup raw barley
¾ cup raw rice

If you are starting with a fresh whole chicken (or chicken parts), season the chicken very liberally with the salt and pepper. It may seem like a lot, but it will cook into the broth. Heat the olive oil, in a 7-8 quart Dutch oven or large soup pot over medium high heat. Sear the seasoned chicken on all sides until golden brown, about 3 minutes per side. (If you are using a chicken carcass, this step is not needed. Simply put the carcass into your pot! You may want to cook a couple of extra boneless chicken breasts separately depending how much meat is left on the carcass so you have enough meat for the soup.)

Add the onions, celery, and stock to the pot. Add enough water to cover the chicken and bouillon cubes. Bring to a boil and reduce to low and let cook for 2-3 hours, stirring occasionally. Using a large spoon, periodically skim the fat and foam off the top of the stock and discard (so the soup is not greasy).

Remove the chicken, which will most likely be falling apart, to a large bowl and let cool.

Add the carrots to the pot and keep at a low boil. (Note—if you are adding rice or barley, they should be added at the same time as the carrots.) Once carrots are tender, about 30 minutes, the chicken should be cool enough to shred with your hands. Add shredded chicken in bite size pieces to the soup along with any of the other "optional" items and cook for 10 minutes more. Stir in parsley just before serving.

Rate It!

grilled corn and chicken chowder
with roasted red pepper and smoky gouda finish

2 large chicken breasts, bone-in and skin on (about 2
  ½-3 pounds.)
3 teaspoons salt
3 teaspoons black pepper
¼ cup olive oil
1 large onion, chopped
3 celery ribs, chopped (about 2 cups)
1 jalapeno, chopped
¼ cup flour
8 cups chicken stock

1 pound baby potatoes, cut into quarters—about
  1-inch pieces (I like to use the tri-color potatoes,
  but any combo will work)
8 ears corn, husks and silks removed
1 large red bell pepper
2 cups light cream
1 cup smoked gouda cheese, shredded (plus more for
  garnish)
½ cup scallions, chopped

Season the chicken breasts on both sides with 1 teaspoon each of the salt and pepper.

Heat the olive oil in a large Dutch oven or stock pot over medium high heat. Add the chicken breasts, skin-side down and sear on all sides until golden, about 6 minutes.

Add the onion, celery, and jalapeno to the pot and stir cooking until vegetables are soft and fragrant. Stir in the flour and cook for 1 minute. Add the chicken stock to the pot, cover, reduce the heat to low, and cook for 1 hour.

Remove the chicken from the pot and set aside to cool. Skim any fat or foam off the top of the stock. Bring the stock back to a low boil and add the potatoes and cook until just tender, about 15 minutes. Continue to skim any excess fat or foam from the top of the stock.

While the potatoes bubble away, heat your grill to medium high heat. Place your corn and red pepper on the hot grill and cover. Cook for 30 minutes, turning every ten minutes until corn is lightly charred and pepper skin is black. Remove from the grill and let cool. Wrap the charred pepper in foil so it can steam and set the corn aside.

When the red pepper is cool enough to handle, remove the charred skin under running water (it will peel off easily). Remove the stem and seeds inside and then chop the pepper into ½-inch pieces. Add them to the pot.

Cut the corn kernels off each cob (quick tip—do this holding the corn inside a large bowl and kernels will not fly all over the place). Add the corn to the chowder.

Remove the skin from the chicken breasts and shred all of the meat off the bones into bite size pieces and add to the pot.... It's getting good now, right??? Season with 1 teaspoon each of the salt and pepper.

Add the light cream and the cheese to the pot and stir until the cheese is melted. Test for seasoning and use as much of the remaining teaspoon each of salt and pepper as needed.

Serve hot garnished with scallions and a sprinkle of shredded gouda cheese.

Rate It!
☆☆☆☆☆

creamy chicken and wild rice soup

This soup is made with bone-in chicken breasts, but can also be made with a chicken carcass. Roast chicken for dinner one night—soup the next!! You can also freeze the carcass and pull directly from your freezer any rainy or snowy day and quickly put together a delicious soup in no time... not to mention your house will smell amazing.

1 tablespoon olive oil
2 ½ pounds bone-in, skin-on chicken breasts
1 teaspoon salt
1 teaspoon black pepper
1 large onion, chopped
3 cups celery, chopped
½ teaspoon dried thyme
½ teaspoon dried basil

½ teaspoon dried oregano
10 cups chicken stock
3 cups carrots, sliced
2 cups raw wild rice
10 ounces mushrooms, sliced
1 pint heavy cream
2 tablespoons flat leaf parsley, chopped

Heat the olive oil in a large soup pot or Dutch oven over medium high heat. Season the chicken liberally with the salt and pepper. Place skin-side down in the hot oil and sear on the first side until golden and fragrant. Flip the breasts and add the onion, celery, thyme, basil, and oregano to the pot and continue to cook, stirring occasionally until the onions and celery begin to soften, about 5 minutes. Add the chicken stock to the pan and bring to a boil. Reduce heat to low, cover and cook for 60-90 minutes, stirring occasionally, until chicken is falling apart.

Remove the chicken from pot and set aside to cool. Add the carrots, rice and mushrooms to the pot, cover and continue to cook over low heat for 30-40 minutes.

Remove the chicken skin and take the meat off the bones and shred into bite-size pieces. Add back into the pot along with the cream and parsley. Bring back up to heat, stirring occasionally for 5 more minutes. Serve garnished with more parsley and crusty bread on the side.

Rate It!

chicken minestrone
with tortellini 3-bean bang up soup

2 tablespoons olive oil
1 large onion, chopped
3 cups celery, chopped into ½-inch pieces
3 cups carrots, chopped into 1-inch pieces
½ pound chorizo sausage, chopped into ½-inch pieces
10 cloves garlic, peeled and chopped
1 small red bell pepper, chopped
3 cups zucchini, chopped into 1-inch half moons
3 tablespoons **Dish off the Block Ciao Bella Italian Spice Blend**
2 teaspoons salt
1 teaspoon black pepper
8 cups chicken stock

1 cup dry red wine
1, 28-ounce can tomato puree
1, 14.5-ounce can chopped tomatoes
2 boneless chicken breasts
½ cup lentils
1, 15-ounce can cannellini beans, drained and rinsed
1, 10.5-ounce can black beans, drained and rinsed
2 cups frozen corn
2 cups frozen cheese tortellini
½ cup fresh basil leaves, chiffonade (plus more for garnish
parmesan cheese for garnish

Heat the olive oil in a 9-10 quart Dutch oven or large soup pot (this makes a lot of soup!). Sauté the onion, celery, carrots, chorizo, garlic, red pepper, and zucchini over medium high heat, adding each in order as you chop them and stirring frequently.

When the vegetables are fragrant and everything has been added, about 8-10 minutes, add the Italian seasoning, salt and pepper to the pan, stirring to coat.

Add the stock, red wine, tomato puree, chopped tomatoes, and chicken breasts to the pan. Bring to a boil and then reduce to a simmer. Add the lentils, cover and cook for 30 minutes.

Add the cannellini beans, black beans, and corn to the pot and remove the chicken breasts to a bowl. Cover and continue to simmer for another 30-40 minutes until chicken is cool enough to shred with your hands.

Shred the chicken into bite size pieces and add the shredded chicken and tortellini to the pot and cook for another 20-30 minutes. Just before serving, stir in the fresh basil.

Serve hot, garnished with more fresh basil and parmesan cheese.

Rate It!
☆☆☆☆☆

one more bite! curried chicken ramen

¼ cup olive oil

1, 4 pound whole chicken cut into pieces (or about 4
   pounds chicken parts bone-in)

3 cups celery chopped (with leaves)

1 medium onion, chopped

1 large leek, chopped (both white and tender green
   parts)

4 large carrots, diced

4 large soft chicken bouillon cubes (or 3 tablespoons
   chicken base)

1 jalapeno pepper, chopped (including seeds)

1 small red bell pepper, chopped

1 small orange bell pepper, chopped

1 teaspoon salt

1 teaspoon black pepper

2 tablespoons curry powder

½ teaspoon red pepper flakes

1, 13.5-ounce can coconut milk

2 cups frozen corn kernels

½ cup fresh cilantro, chopped

THE RAMEN:

3 cups flour

1 teaspoon salt

1 teaspoon baking soda

2 eggs, beaten + ½ cup warm water

In a 5-6 quart stock pot or Dutch oven, heat olive oil over medium high heat. Season chicken parts liberally with salt and pepper on both sides and set in hot oil to sear, about 3 minutes per side. Add the celery, onion, leeks, and carrots to the pot. Continue cooking until the vegetables are fragrant and start to brown. Add bouillon cubes and enough water to cover the chicken and bring to a low boil. Let cook for about 20 minutes until fragrant and the chicken is cooked through. Remove the chicken and set aside to cool. Skim any excess fat off the top of the stock with a large spoon.

Add the jalapeno, red, and orange peppers to the stock and let cook on a low boil for another 10 minutes until carrots are fork tender.

While the soup is bubbling away, prepare the ramen dough. Mix flour, salt and baking soda on the counter and create a 'well' in the center of the flour. Place egg and water mixture in the well and slowly incorporate into the flour with a fork, pulling flour from the outside in until dough begins to come together. Knead until smooth. Let rest in the refrigerator for 20 minutes.

Flour the dough generously and roll it out to the 3 setting on your pasta roller. Cut the dough in half so you have two sheets of dough a little over 1 foot long and flour generously again. Use the spaghetti attachment to cut the pasta into long thin noodles, dusting them with flour as they are cut to keep them from sticking together.

Shred the chicken into bit size pieces and add to the pot along with salt, pepper, curry powder, red pepper flakes, coconut milk, and corn. Continue to cook over medium heat allowing all of the flavors to combine and meld into the broth. About 3 minutes before serving add the ramen noodles and cilantro, reserving 2 table-spoons for garnish. Cook until pasta is curled and tender. Serve steaming hot in bowls garnished with fresh chopped cilantro.

Rate It!
☆☆☆☆☆

pucker up lemony chicken orzo soup

2 tablespoons olive oil
2-2 ½ pounds chicken breasts (bone-in and skin on)
1 ½ teaspoon salt
1 ½ teaspoon black pepper
1 large onion, chopped
3 cups celery, chopped into ½-inch pieces
5 garlic cloves, chopped
6 slices of ginger root, ⅛-inch thick
2 ½ lemons, cut in half crosswise (5 halves total)
12 sprigs of thyme, bunch tied together with kitchen string

8 cups chicken stock
2-3 cups water
2 cups carrots, sliced about ¼-inch thick
¾ cup uncooked orzo pasta
5 ounces baby spinach/baby kale combo
½ cup flat leaf parsley, chopped (plus more for garnish)
3 eggs
Parmesan cheese, served on the side

Heat olive oil in a large Dutch oven or stock pot over medium high heat. Season the chicken breasts with 1 teaspoon each of the salt and pepper. Place them skin side down into the hot oil. Let cook for about 2 minutes per side until golden and fragrant.

Add the onions and celery to the pot and continue to cook, stirring frequently, until the onions begin to soften. Add the garlic and ginger to the pan and cook for 2 more minutes, stirring frequently.

Squeeze 4 of the lemon halves into the pot and then place the squeezed rinds into the pot and continue to cook for 3 more minutes. Add the thyme, chicken stock, and water to the pot. Bring to a boil, reduce to a simmer and cover. Cook for 1 hour.

Remove the chicken from the pot and let cool. Discard the lemon rinds. Bring the soup back to a low boil. Add the carrots and orzo to the pot and cook for 20-30 minutes until carrots are tender.

Shred the chicken into bite size pieces and add back into the soup (discard skin and bones) along with the greens, parsley, and remaining ½ teaspoon each of salt and pepper.

Squeeze the juice from the remaining lemon half into a large bowl. Add the rind to the soup pot.

Add the 3 eggs to the bowl with the lemon juice and whisk the eggs until well beaten. Take ½ cup of the hot stock from the pot and VERY SLOWLY add to the beaten eggs, whisking constantly. This will 'temper' the eggs so that when you add them into the soup they do not scramble.

As soon as stock is incorporated into the eggs, add the contents of the eggs and stock into the soup and continue to stir constantly for 3 minutes until a creamy broth forms and the eggs are completely incorporated. The soup will look light yellow, creamy, and luscious!

Serve immediately garnished with more parsley and parmesan cheese.

Rate It!
☆☆☆☆☆

chicken, sweet potato, and 3 pepper chowder
with a hint of heat

2 tablespoons olive oil
1 small onion, chopped (about 1 cup)
1 small leek, chopped white and light green
    parts (about 1 cup)
2 cups chopped celery
1 jalapeno, chopped including the seeds
1 tablespoon fresh ginger root, minced
6 cloves garlic, chopped
1 small green pepper, chopped (about 1 cup)
1 small red pepper, chopped (about 1 cup)
3 carrots, chopped

1 large sweet potato, peeled and chopped into
    bite size pieces (about 2 ½ cups)
2 teaspoons salt
2 teaspoons **Dish off the Block Superbly Herby
    Spice Blend**
4 cups chicken stock
1 large boneless chicken breast
1 ½ cups zucchini, shredded
1 cup heavy cream
¼ cup fresh basil or parsley, chopped for garnish

Heat the olive oil in a large Dutch oven or soup pot over medium high heat. Add the onions, leeks, celery, jalapeno, ginger, and garlic to the pan. Cook for 3-4 minutes until the veggies begin to soften and are fragrant.

Add the red and green peppers, carrots, sweet potatoes, salt, and Superbly Herby Seasoning to the pan. Continue to cook for another 5 minutes, stirring frequently.

Pour in the chicken stock and add the full chicken breast to the pot. Bring everything to a boil and then turn the heat down and cook on a low boil for 15-20 minutes until the carrots and sweet potatoes are tender when pierced with a fork.

Remove the chicken breast and let it cool on a cutting board until you can handle it with your fingers.

Add the zucchini and the heavy cream to the pot and continue cooking on a simmer while your chicken cools, about 10 minutes.

Shred the chicken into bite size pieces and add it back to the pot. Cook for another 5-10 minutes. Serve hot in bowls with crusty bread or crostini for dipping.

Rate It!
☆☆☆☆☆

SALADS

Salads

old school chicken salad

One of my favorite tips is to buy boneless chicken breasts in bulk when they are on sale, cook them, shred or chop, and freeze for future use. To cook, place the chicken breasts in a large deep skillet or pot and cover with water. Bring to a boil and let cook for 20-30 minutes until just cooked through. Let cool and shred or chop into bite size pieces. Place the shredded chicken in large Ziploc™ bags in measured portions of 3 or 4 cups. Now, you have cooked chicken at your fingertips to use in casseroles, soups, and salads on busy weeknights with no prep needed!

4 cups chicken breast, cooked and shredded into bite size pieces (packed cups)
1 cup fresh celery, finely chopped including the leaves
2 cups Hellmann's Light mayonnaise
1 teaspoon Dijon mustard
1 teaspoon salt
1 teaspoon black pepper
1 teaspoon celery seed
1 tablespoon brown sugar, packed

Mix all ingredients together in a large bowl until well combined and coated. Best if it sits for a few hours or overnight so flavors meld.

Serve on crusty bread with lettuce, tomatoes, and red onion slices or on top of a green salad... or just a fork!

Rate It!

☆☆☆☆☆

grilled honey mustard chicken salad
with pears and funky gorgonzola

THE MARINADE/DRESSING:

½ cup olive oil
½ cup honey
¼ cup whole grain mustard

1 tablespoon Dijon mustard
⅓ cup apple cider vinegar

2-3 boneless, skinless chicken breasts (about 1 pound)
1 teaspoon salt
1 teaspoon black pepper
8 ounces mixed greens with baby spinach

2 pears, pitted and sliced into ½-inch wedges
½ cup candied pecans
½ cup dried cranberries
½ cup gorgonzola cheese

Combine all of the marinade/dressing ingredients in a large jar and shake until creamy and emulsified.

Season chicken breasts with salt and pepper. Place in a small bowl and cover with ⅓ cup of the marinade and cover with plastic wrap. Let sit for at least 3 hours or, even better, overnight.

Heat grill to medium high. Place marinated breasts on the grill and cook about 8-10 minutes per side until cooked through—internal temp at thickest part should be about 155-165 degrees—note chicken will keep cooking after you remove it from grill, cover with foil and let rest for 20 minutes. Chicken should be just cooked through and juices should run clear when you cut into it.

Place the greens on a platter (or individual plates) and top with pears. Cut the chicken against the grain and on a bias in ½-inch slices. Fan over the pears. Top with the nuts, cranberries, and gorgonzola. Drizzle with the dressing and toss to combine. Serve immediately when dressed.

Note—you will have extra dressing to enjoy on future salads or to use as a marinade.

Rate It!
☆☆☆☆

curried chicken and apple salad

Not a fan of curry? You will be after having this salad. This is a great way to introduce the smoky, earthy curry essence into your diet. It beautifully complements the bright crisp apples and sweet pop from the grapes.

3 cups boneless chicken breast, cooked and shredded into bite size pieces (packed cups)

1 cup celery, finely diced including leaves

1 ½ cups Hellmann's Light mayonnaise

3 teaspoons curry powder

2 large, firm apples chopped into ½-inch dice (skin on—I like Delicious or Honey Crisp)

1 cup seedless grapes, sliced in half

½ teaspoon salt

½ teaspoon black pepper

1 teaspoon Dijon mustard

1 tablespoon brown sugar

Juice of one lemon

Mix all ingredients together in a large bowl. Toss well to combine and coat. Serve over mixed greens or pack in a container for the best lunch on the beach or at the office (I prefer the beach, of course)!

Rate It!

☆☆☆☆

asian noodle salad with chicken and rainbow veggies

1 pound linguine or spaghetti, cooked al dente

¼ cup olive oil

2 cup snow peas, stringed

3 cups cooked chicken breast, shredded (or cooked shrimp)

3 scallions, white and green parts sliced thin

⅓ cup cilantro leaves, chopped

1 red bell pepper, julienned and cut into about 3-inch strips

1 yellow bell pepper, julienned and cut into about 3-inch strips

1 orange bell pepper, julienned and cut into about 3-inch strips

1 ½ cups edamame beans, cooked and shelled

THE DRESSING:

¾ cup soy sauce

¼ cup creamy peanut butter

¼ cup rice vinegar

1 tablespoon sesame oil

1 tablespoon sugar

1 teaspoon fresh ginger root, grated or finely minced

1 jalapeno, minced

1 teaspoon black pepper

Place cooked linguini in a large bowl and toss with the olive oil to keep it from sticking together while you prepare the rest of the ingredients.

Place snow peas in a small pot of boiling water until bright green and crisp tender, about 30 seconds. Rinse with cold water and drain well. Add to the bowl with the noodles along with all of the other salad ingredients.

Combine all of the dressing ingredients in a small bowl and whisk vigorously until a smooth dressing forms. Add dressing to the bowl and mix thoroughly. I find it easiest to use my hands for this. Served chilled or at room temperature.

Rate It!
☆☆☆☆☆

dreamy grilled chicken, cranberry, and gorgonzola pasta salad

THE MARINADE:

½ cup olive oil
¼ cup Hellmann's Light mayonnaise
½ cup honey
¼ cup whole grain mustard
1 tablespoon Dijon mustard

⅓ cup apple cider vinegar
2-3 boneless, skinless chicken breasts (about 1 ½
    pounds)
1 teaspoon salt
1 teaspoon black pepper

THE DRESSING:

1 ½ cups Hellmann's Light mayonnaise
¼ cup whole grain mustard
1 tablespoon brown sugar, packed

½ cup cider vinegar
1 teaspoon salt
1 teaspoon black pepper

THE SALAD:

1 pound rotini pasta, cooked al dente according to
    package directions
1 ½ cups dried cranberries
1 cup bacon, cooked crisp and chopped

2 cups green grapes, cut in half
½ cup flat leaf parsley, chopped
2 cups gorgonzola cheese, crumbled
1 ½ cups walnuts, rough chopped

Combine all of the marinade ingredients in a medium bowl. Coat the chicken breasts in the marinade and let sit for at least 2 hours or overnight.

Preheat grill to medium high (about 450 degrees). Add the marinated breasts to the hot grill and cook about 5-7 minutes per side (depending on thickness) until the internal temperature reaches 160 degrees. Set aside and cover with foil to rest while you prepare the rest of the salad.

Combine all of the dressing ingredients in a small bowl and whisk to combine.

In a large bowl, combine the pasta, cranberries, bacon, grapes, parsley, and gorgonzola.

Toast the nuts in a dry frying pan stirring occasionally for 3-5 minutes until lightly browned and fragrant. Add to the salad bowl.

Chop the chicken into 1-inch cubes and add to the salad along with the dressing. Toss everything to combine. Serve at room temperature or cold.

Rate It!
☆☆☆☆

chicken cobb salad

THE DRESSING:

½ cup olive oil

¼ cup red wine vinegar

¼ cup honey

¼ cup grainy mustard

¼ teaspoon salt

½ teaspoon black pepper

THE SALAD:

2 chicken breasts, boneless and skinless

1 head romaine lettuce, chopped

1 cup grape tomatoes, cut in half

2 avocados, pitted and sliced

6 eggs, hard boiled, peeled and sliced

½ pound bacon, cooked crisp and chopped

½ cup crumbled gorgonzola or blue cheese

½ cup red onion, chopped

Combine all of the dressing ingredients in a large jar and shake well to combine (or whisk them together in a small bowl until emulsified).

Place the chicken breasts in a large Ziploc™ bag with ¼ cup of the dressing and let marinate for 3 hours or overnight. Heat your grill or a grill pan to medium high heat. Place the marinated chicken on the hot grill and cook, about 4-5 minutes per side until just cooked through and chicken is 160 degrees internally. Cover with foil and set aside to rest for at least 15 minutes.

Layer the remaining ingredients either on a platter or in individual bowls. Slice the chicken crosswise into thin strips and layer on top of the salad. Drizzle the dressing over the top.

Rate It!

☆☆☆☆☆

chicken waldorf salad

Waldorf Salad is named for the Waldorf Astoria Hotel in New York City. The story goes that it was created by the Maitre d'hotel (NOT the head chef) in 1896. The original recipe was made with only apples, celery, and mayonnaise. Nuts and grapes were added in later iterations and the addition of chicken breast makes this the perfect entrée salad.

3 cups apples, cored and chopped into 1-inch chunks (I like a combo of Honey Crisp and Granny Smith, but any firm, crisp apples will work)

1 cup seedless grapes, cut in half

1 cup celery, chopped

2 packed cups chicken breast, cooked and shredded

1 cup walnuts, rough chopped and lightly toasted

1 cup Hellmann's Light mayonnaise

1 teaspoon salt

1 teaspoon black pepper

1 tablespoon brown sugar

2 tablespoons lemon juice

Romaine lettuce leaves

Combine all of the ingredients together in a large bowl and mix thoroughly. Let sit for a couple of hours before serving and toss again just before you are ready to serve. Serve over Romaine lettuce leaves

This recipe also doubles beautifully for a buffet or brunch!

Rate It!
☆☆☆☆

MAIN COURSES

Main Courses

chicken pot pie

THE CRUST:

½ teaspoon salt
3 cups flour
½ cup cold shortening
½ cup cold butter

1 egg
8-10 tablespoons ice water
2 teaspoons white vinegar

Mix the flour and salt in a large bowl.

Cut in shortening and butter with a pastry blender until the mixture is crumbly and resembles coarse meal.

Beat the egg, vinegar, and 8 tablespoons of ice water together in a separate bowl.

Using a fork, add the egg mixture to the dry ingredients and combine until the dough begins to come together. Add additional 2 tablespoons of water as needed. Turn onto the counter and pull the pieces together, pressing the dough together firmly with your hands to combine and form a ball. Do not overwork the dough. The consistency should hold together but still have visible chunks of butter and shortening in the dough. This will make a flaky crust.

Break dough into 2 even pieces and form each into a disc. Wrap each disc in plastic wrap and chill for at least 2 hours or overnight.

THE FILLING:

4 cups carrots, chopped into
    ½-inch dice (about 6-8 large
    carrots)
¾ cup butter or margarine
¾ cup flour
2 cups strong chicken broth
    (enhance it with chicken
    bouillon cubes if needed)

3 cups milk
4 cups chicken breast, cooked and
    shredded into bite size pieces
2 cups frozen peas
1 teaspoon black pepper
½ teaspoon salt
1 egg yolk

Melt butter in a large deep skillet and cook carrots, stirring freqently. Cover the pan while cooking, about 8-10 minutes, until tender when pierced with a fork.

Stir flour into carrots and cook for one minute, stirring constantly allowing butter to absorb. Gradually add chicken broth, followed by the milk, stirring constantly, until a rich thick gravy forms. Stir in chicken and frozen peas. Remove from heat and let cool to room temperature. You can make the filling in advance and keep in the refrigerator, but bring back to room temperature before assembling the pie.

Remove dough from the refrigerator and roll each disc into a 13-14-inch circle. Place one crust into a 10-inch pie plate allowing excess crust to drape over the edge.

Spoon filling into the pie plate and top with the second crust. Crimp edges together all around to seal. I like to press with a fork after crimping for a good seal. Cut a few air vents in the top of the crust. Combine the egg yolk with 1 teaspoon of water and brush the egg wash all over the crust.

Bake at 350 degrees for 1 hour or until filling begins to bubble out of the crust and crust is golden brown. Let set for 10 minutes and dig in!

Serves 6-8

Rate It!
☆☆☆☆☆

chicken parm spaghetti squash boats

1 spaghetti squash (about 3 pounds)
½ cup + 2 tablespoons olive oil, divided
2 teaspoons salt
2 teaspoons black pepper
2 boneless, skinless chicken breasts
    (about 1 ¼-1 ½ pounds)
1 egg, beaten
¼ cup Italian seasoned breadcrumbs

¾ cup panko breadcrumbs
1 cup parmesan cheese
3 tablespoons butter, softened
1 ½ cups marinara or spaghetti sauce
1 cup mozzarella cheese
1 tablespoon fresh chopped parsley
1 tablespoon fresh chopped basil

Preheat oven to 375 degrees. Cut the spaghetti squash in half lengthwise and scrape out the seeds in the center with a spoon and discard. Drizzle 2 tablespoons of the olive oil over the cut side of the squash and sprinkle with 1 teaspoon each of the salt and pepper. Place cut-side down on a foil-lined cookie sheet. Bake for 45 minutes or an hour, until tender when pierced with a fork. Let cool for 10 minutes until you can handle with your hands.

While the squash is cooking, cut the chicken into cubes, about 2-3-inches.

Add 1 teaspoon each of salt and pepper to your beaten eggs and toss the chicken cubes in the egg to coat.

Combine the Italian breadcrumbs with ½ cup of the panko crumbs, and ¼ cup of the Parmesan in a pie plate or shallow baking dish.

Heat ¼-inch of olive oil to cover the bottom of a large non-stick skillet over medium high heat. Coat the egg covered chicken cubes in the breadcrumb mixture and place in the hot oil. Brown on all sides and remove from pan to a plate covered with paper towels to absorb any excess oil. Do not worry if the chicken is slightly underdone as it will go in the oven and continue cooking.

Using a fork, shred the squash and scoop into a large bowl, keeping the shells intact. Toss the squash with ½ cup of the parmesan cheese and the butter and put back into the shells. Top the squash in each shell with half of the marinara sauce. Top with the chicken cubes followed by the rest of the sauce. Sprinkle ½ cup of the mozzarella cheese on each 'boat'.

Combine the final ¼ each of panko and parmesan with parsley and 2 teaspoons of olive oil in a small bowl. Sprinkle this mixture over the top of each squash. Bake for 20-30 minutes until browned, melty, and bubbly.

Garnish with fresh basil and mangia!!

Serves 4-6

Rate It!
☆☆☆☆☆

sesame chicken
with ginger shitake cream sauce

4 large, boneless skinless chicken breasts
1 teaspoon salt
1 teaspoon black pepper
½ cup white sesame seeds
¼ cup black sesame seeds
3 tablespoons peanut oil
1 tablespoon butter
3 tablespoons fresh ginger root, minced

6 large garlic cloves, chopped
16 ounces shitake mushrooms, stems discarded and
    caps sliced
3 tablespoons soy sauce
2 cups heavy whipping cream
2 tablespoons prepared wasabi mustard
3 cups cooked sushi rice

Place chicken breasts, one at a time, in a large Ziploc™ bag and pound with a mallet until each breast is ½-inch even thickness throughout. Season each breast on both sides with salt and pepper. Combine white and black sesame seeds in a small bowl and gently press 1 tablespoon of the mixture onto both sides of each breast.

Heat the peanut oil in a large skillet and sauté each chicken breast over medium heat until lightly browned on both sides and just cooked through. Remove from pan and cover with foil to keep warm.

Melt the tablespoon of butter in the same pan and add the ginger and garlic. Sauté over medium heat for one minute until fragrant. Add mushrooms and soy sauce and cook for another three minutes. Add cream and wasabi and bring to a boil, stirring frequently for 5-7 minutes until the sauce thickens and coats the back of a spoon.

Prepare sushi rice according to package directions for six ½ cup servings.

Place ½ cup of the sushi rice in a small ramekin and unmold on each plate. Top with one chicken breast and lots of yummy sauce. If the breasts are large, cut in half for smaller portion size.

Garnish with chopped scallions.

Serves 4-6

Rate It!

chicken cordon bleu casserole

This easy casserole encompasses all of the flavors in the traditional Swiss dish Cordon Bleu which is pounded veal or chicken stuffed with ham and Swiss cheese, breaded and fried. All of the flavor without all the fuss.

8 cups boneless chicken breast, cooked and chopped into 2-inch cubes (about 4 large breasts)
1, 8 ounce ham steak, cut into ½-inch cubes
2 ½ cups shredded Swiss cheese (good quality like Jarlsberg or Gruyere)
3 teaspoons fresh thyme leaves, stemmed
½ teaspoon black pepper, divided

2 cups panko breadcrumbs
6 tablespoons butter, divided
2 tablespoons flour
2 cups chicken stock
1 tablespoon whole grain mustard
2 teaspoons Dijon mustard
1 tablespoon honey
1 cup light cream

Preheat oven to 350 degrees.

Spray a 9x13-inch casserole dish with non-stick cooking spray. Layer 4 cups of the chicken breast in the bottom of the pan, followed by half of the ham, 1 cup of the cheese, 1 teaspoon of the thyme leaves, ¼ teaspoon black pepper, and 1 cup of the panko.

Repeat with the remaining 4 cups of chicken, the rest of the ham, cheese, and black pepper.

In a large sauce pan melt 2 tablespoons of the butter. Add flour and whisk for one minute until smooth and bubbly. Slowly whisk in the chicken stock, both mustards, and honey followed by light cream. Continue to whisk over medium heat until a velvety sauce forms. Pour this sauce evenly over the casserole letting it seep into all of the cracks and crevices.

Melt the remaining 4 tablespoons butter in another large sauce pan. Add the remaining 1 cup panko and remaining thyme leaves. Stir to coat and cook for one minute until crumbs begin to lightly brown. Spread the buttered crumbs evenly over the top of the casserole.

Bake for 30 minutes until browned and bubbly. Serve with a simple green salad with light vinaigrette.

Serves 8

Rate It!
☆☆☆☆

princess chicken and shrimp pasta
with asparagus and mushroom cream sauce

THE CHICKEN:

1 ½ pounds boneless chicken breasts
1 cup flour
1 teaspoon salt
1 teaspoon black pepper

1 teaspoon garlic powder
4 tablespoons butter
2 tablespoons olive oil

THE SAUCE:

1 medium onion, chopped
8 large garlic cloves, chopped
8 ounces mushrooms, rough chopped
2 cups heavy cream
½ cup dry white wine
2 tablespoons sherry

½ teaspoon salt
1 teaspoon black pepper
1 tablespoon tomato paste
*1 bunch asparagus, woody ends removed and
    chopped into 3-4-inch pieces (about 2 cups)*

THE SHRIMP:

3 tablespoons butter
12 ounces large raw shrimp, peeled and deveined

THE GARNISH:

⅓ cup fresh flat leaf parsley, chopped
½ cup grated parmesan cheese (on side for sprinkling)

1 pound fresh fettuccini pasta, cooked al dente

Butterfly each chicken breast (by cutting in half horizontally) to make 2 thin cutlets. Then, place each cutlet into a large Ziploc™ bag and pound with a meat pounder until an even ¼-inch thickness all over. If the pieces are large, you may want to cut them in half to make them easier to work with.

Combine the flour, salt, pepper, and garlic powder in a shallow baking dish or pie plate. Dredge the chicken cutlets in the seasoned flour.

Heat the butter and olive oil in a large deep skillet over medium high heat. Sauté the chicken breasts until lightly browned on both sides and just cooked through, about 1-2 minutes per side. Remove to a platter and cover with foil to keep warm. Reserve the pan drippings.

Add the onion and garlic to the pan drippings and sauté over medium heat until soft and fragrant. Add the mushrooms to the pan and continue to cook until mushrooms are soft and begin to release some of their moisture. Add the heavy cream, wine, sherry, salt, and pepper to the pan and bring to a low boil, stirring frequently. Let cook for 5-7 minutes, stirring occasionally until sauce has reduced and coats the

Rate It!
☆☆☆☆☆

back of a spoon. Whisk in the tomato paste and add the asparagus to the sauce. Let cook for another minute while you prepare the shrimp. Note—you want the asparagus to be crisp tender so they only need to cook for 1-2 minutes in the sauce.

To prepare the shrimp, melt the butter in a medium sauce pan over medium high heat. If there is excess liquid in the bag with the shrimp, drain it directly into the cream sauce and then add the shrimp to the hot butter. Sauté until just pink. Add the shrimp and any pan drippings into the cream sauce as well and cook for one more minute, stirring to combine and allowing the sauce to further thicken and reduce.

Add the cooked pasta directly into your sauce along with the chicken and toss everything together to evenly coat. Serve in pasta bowls, garnished with parsley and parmesan cheese.

Serves 6-8

herby chicken thighs
in mushroom parmesan cream sauce

6 chicken thighs, bone-in, skin-on (about 1 ½ pounds)

2 teaspoons salt

2 teaspoons black pepper

2 teaspoons garlic powder

2 tablespoons fresh rosemary, leaves stemmed and chopped

3 tablespoons olive oil

1 large onion, chopped

12 sprigs of thyme, tied with kitchen string

8 ounces cremini mushrooms, sliced

5 garlic cloves, chopped

¾ cup dry white wine

½ cup chicken stock

2 cups heavy cream

1 cup grated parmesan cheese

1 pound angel hair pasta, cooked al dente

⅓ cup chopped parsley

Preheat oven to 400 degrees.

Trim any excess fat from the chicken thighs.

Combine the salt, pepper, garlic powder, and rosemary in a small bowl. Season the thighs liberally on both sides with the rosemary mixture, pressing to adhere.

Heat olive oil in a large, deep, oven proof skillet over medium high heat. When the oil is very hot, place the thighs in the pan, skin side down. Sear until the skin is crispy and golden brown, about 3-4 minutes. Flip over and cook for 2 minutes on the other side. Remove from the pan and set aside (note—chicken will not be completely cooked through yet).

Add the onion to the pan drippings along with the thyme and sauté until soft and fragrant. Add the mushrooms and garlic to the pan and cook, stirring frequently until the mushrooms are soft and lightly browned.

Add the wine and chicken stock to the pan and bring to a boil and cook for 2 minutes, letting the liquid reduce, stirring occasionally. Add the heavy cream to the pan and cook for 2 more minutes, letting the sauce thicken. Slowly, add the parmesan cheese, about 2 tablespoons at a time stirring constantly to incorporate it into the sauce (if you add it all at once, you will have a big clump of parmesan in your sauce—no bueno!).

Place the chicken thighs back into the pan, nestled into the sauce but leave the skin exposed so it remains crispy. Transfer the pan to the oven and bake, uncovered for 10-20 minutes until the chicken is cooked through.

Serve one thigh over the angel hair pasta, drizzled with luscious sauce and garnished with parsley.

Serves 6

Rate It!

fajita pie

This was one of my first recipe creations and still one of the top dishes requested by my high school girlfriends. Check out the video for step by step instructions and order some **Dish off the Block Ragin' Cajun Spice Blend** to turn up the heat!

⅓ + ¼ cup olive oil, divided
3 medium to large green peppers, sliced in strips
3 large yellow onions, sliced in strips
1 jalapeno chopped
1 red bell pepper, sliced in strips
1 teaspoon salt
½ teaspoon black pepper
4 chicken breast halves, cooked and shredded into bite-size pieces (about 5 cups)

2 tablespoons **Dish off the Block Ragin' Cajun Spice Blend**
3 cups medium spicy salsa
6, 8-10-inch flour tortillas
2 cups tomatoes, chopped (or 1 pint grape tomatoes cut in half)
5 cups shredded cheddar or Mexican blend cheese
1, 2.5 ounce can sliced black olives, drained
3 tablespoons cilantro, chopped for garnish
Sour cream served on the side

Heat ⅓ cup of olive oil in a large deep skillet over medium heat. Sauté green peppers, onions, and jalapeno until they begin to soften. Add red bell peppers, salt and pepper and continue to cook, stirring frequently, until they are soft and lightly caramelized, about 10-15 minutes. Remove from pan, but save the pan drippings.

Combine chicken and **Dish off the Block Ragin' Cajun Spice Blend** with the pan drippings and additional ¼ cup olive oil and sauté until the chicken is well-coated with the spices.

Spray a 9x13-inch baking dish with non-stick spray. Spread ½ cup of salsa on bottom of the baking dish and top with 2 tortillas to cover the bottom of pan.

Spread ½ cup of salsa on top of tortillas followed by ⅓ of the chicken, ⅓ of the onions & peppers, ¼ of tomatoes, 1 ¼ cups of the cheese, and salsa again. Top with another two tortillas and repeat layers two more times. Your top layer will end with tortillas, salsa, cheese, tomatoes, and the black olives.

Bake at 375 degrees for 25-30 minutes until hot and bubbly!

Let rest 5 minutes after you take it out of the oven to set. Serve with sour cream on the side and garnish with chopped cilantro.

Serves 6-8

Rate It!

bacon ranch chicken and avocado pizza

This pizza can be cooked on a large sheet pan, but a pizza stone makes the crispiest crust!

Pizza dough for one crust (recipe page 93)
¼ cup cornmeal
3 tablespoons ranch dressing
2 cups Colby Jack cheese (or Cheddar Jack)
1 ½ cups cooked chicken breast, shredded into bite size pieces

6 strips bacon, cooked (not too crisp since they will cook again) and rough chopped
1 cup grape tomatoes, cut in half
¼ cup scallions, chopped
1 avocado, chopped into 1-inch chunks
½ teaspoon black pepper
1 cup baby arugula greens
2 teaspoons olive oil

Preheat oven to 425 degrees. Place pizza stone in the oven and let heat for at least 30 minutes.

Shape the pizza dough into a 12-14-inch round. Spread cornmeal on a pizza peel or large baking sheet with no lip. This will allow you to easily transfer the pizza onto the baking stone in the oven. Arrange the dough on top of the cornmeal (or if you are cooking on a baking sheet with no stone, just arrange the dough on the baking sheet).

Spread half of the ranch dressing evenly over the dough. Top with 1 cup of the cheese.

Mix remaining ranch dressing with the chicken in a small bowl and evenly layer the chicken on the dough. Sprinkle another ½ cup of the cheese over the chicken.

Follow by evenly layering the bacon, tomatoes, scallions, and remaining ½ cup of cheese. Slide the pizza off the peel and onto the stone in the oven. Bake for 14 minutes until browned and bubbly. Remove from the oven using the peel.

Top the hot pizza with avocado and season with the black pepper. Toss the arugula with olive oil and mound the salad in the middle of the pie. Slice and devour!

Serves 4-6

Rate It!
☆☆☆☆

pizza dough

Serves 4-6

2 tablespoons olive oil (plus 2 teaspoons to oil the bowl)
1 tablespoon honey
1 ½ cups warm water (115 degrees)
1 packet yeast
2 teaspoons salt
3 ½-4 cups flour

Place olive oil, honey, and water into the bowl of a stand mixer. Stir to dissolve honey into the water (so it doesn't stick to the bottom of the bowl). Sprinkle the yeast on top of the liquid mixture, stir, and let sit for 5-10 minutes until yeast becomes foamy. Add salt and 2 ½ cups of the flour. Mix using the dough hook attachment. Gradually add as much of the remaining flour as needed until a ball forms. Empty dough onto a floured countertop and knead for 10-15 minutes until dough is smooth and elastic adding flour as needed if sticky.

Place dough in a greased bowl and cover with a clean kitchen towel. Let rise in a warm spot for 1 hour until doubled in bulk. Knead dough briefly and divide into 2 equal parts and form balls. Let rest for 30 minutes under a clean kitchen towel. If you are not using both balls, refrigerate each ball in a plastic bag sprayed with cooking spray for up to 5 days.

Rate It!
★★★★★

pecan-crusted chicken stuffed with bacon, dates, and goat cheese
topped with a maple dijon cream sauce

4-6 boneless, skinless chicken breast halves
   (approx. 2.5-3 pounds)
2 eggs
1 cup pecans, chopped fine
2 tablespoons flour
3 tablespoons brown sugar
½ cup panko breadcrumbs

¾ cup bacon, cooked crisp and chopped
¾ cup chopped dates
11 ounce bar goat cheese, softened
1 teaspoon salt
1 teaspoon black pepper
3 tablespoons vegetable oil
2 tablespoons butter

THE SAUCE:

½ cup maple syrup
1 ½ cup heavy cream
2 teaspoons Dijon mustard

Preheat oven to 350 degrees. Pound each chicken breast half to even ½-inch thickness all over. Set aside.

Create a breading station. Beat the eggs in a pie plate or shallow baking dish. In another shallow dish, mix pecans, flour, brown sugar, and panko.

In a medium bowl, cream together the bacon, dates, and goat cheese. Place in the fridge for 15-20 minutes after it is creamed.

Season the flattened chicken breasts (on the non-smooth side) with salt and pepper. Divide the goat cheese filling evenly among the chicken breasts and place in the center of each. Roll the ends over the filling and use toothpicks if needed to hold them together.

Heat oil and butter in a large non-stick skillet over medium heat. Dip each roll in the egg to coat, letting excess drip off. Then, press into the pecan mixture to adhere. Coat fully and gingerly place in the hot pan. The nut crust is a little fragile so just take care when cooking them. Let cook about 1 minute per side and gingerly turn with tongs, so crust does not come off, until well browned on all sides. Chicken will not be cooked through. Place the browned rolls in a 9x13-inch baking dish, seam side down, and sprinkle any remaining nuts and sugar on the top of the rolls, as well as any that may have fallen off during cooking. Bake in the oven for 20 minutes until chicken is just cooked through.

To make the sauce, mix the maple syrup, heavy cream, and Dijon in a small saucepan. Bring to a light boil over medium heat, reduce to low and continue to lightly boil, whisking occasionally for about 10 minutes, until the sauce is reduced by half and coats the back of a spoon.

Serve one breast sliced into medallions and topped with the sauce. I like rice pilaf and peas or a small green salad on the side.

Serves 4-6

Rate It!
☆☆☆☆☆

chicken, wild mushroom, and wild rice casserole
a walk on the wild side...

6 tablespoons butter, divided
2 tablespoons olive oil
1 ¼ cups carrots, peeled and cut into ½-inch dice
1 ¼ cups celery, chopped into ½-inch pieces
1 large onion, chopped
1 cup red bell pepper, chopped
1 pound wild mushroom mix, sliced (any combo shitake, cremini, oyster, etc...)
1 tablespoon fresh rosemary leaves, stemmed and chopped
1 tablespoon fresh thyme leaves, stemmed
½ cup flour

2 cups chicken stock
1 cup light cream
½ cup milk
1 ½ teaspoons salt
2 teaspoons black pepper
4 cups cooked boneless chicken breast, shredded into bite-size pieces
3 ⅓ cups wild rice blend, cooked according to package directions (about 1 ½ cups raw rice)
3 cups Jarlsberg or good quality Swiss cheese
1 cup panko breadcrumbs

Preheat oven to 350 degrees.

Melt 4 tablespoons of the butter and the oil in a large deep skillet over medium high heat. Add the carrots, celery, onion, and red pepper to the pan and cook for 5-7 minutes, stirring frequently until the carrots are just fork tender. Add the mushrooms, rosemary, and thyme to the pan and continue cooking for 4-5 minutes until the mushrooms release their juices and vegetables begin to lightly brown.

Add the flour to the pan and stir until the flour is all absorbed and the mixture is dry, about 2 minutes. Add the chicken stock and stir until thick. Add the cream and milk and continue stirring until a velvety sauce forms. Season with the salt and pepper.

Fold in the chicken, cooked rice, and 1 cup of the shredded cheese. Pour half of mixture into a 9x13-inch baking dish prepared with non-stick spray. Top with 1 cup of the remaining shredded cheese. Place the rest of the mixture in the pan and finish with the remaining cup of shredded cheese.

Combine the panko and remaining 2 tablespoons butter in a large sauce pan and cook over medium heat, stirring until lightly browned. Spread over the top of the casserole. Bake for 25-30 minutes until browned and bubbly. Garnish with thyme sprigs.

Serves 6-8

Rate It!
☆☆☆☆☆

chicken a la king

5 tablespoons butter
10 ounces white mushrooms, sliced
1 small green pepper, chopped
¼ cup flour
½ teaspoon salt
½ teaspoon black pepper

2 cups boneless chicken breast, cooked and
    shredded into bite-sized pieces
1 cup chicken broth
1 cup milk
1, 4 ounce jar chopped pimentos
1 cup frozen peas, thawed

Heat butter in a large deep skillet over medium high heat. Sauté mushrooms and peppers in butter until tender, about 5 minutes. Add flour, salt, and pepper to the pan to form a roux. Cook for 1 minute, stirring constantly.

Gradually add the broth and milk, still stirring as the sauce thickens, about 4 minutes. Stir in the chicken, pimentos, and peas once the sauce has reached a thick gravy consistency.

Serve hot over rice, toast, or mashed potatoes.

Serves 4-6

Rate It!
☆☆☆☆

neptune's stuffed chicken

8 chicken breast halves, about 3 pounds
¾ cup butter (1 ½ sticks)
1 small onion, chopped
½ cup celery, minced
1 pound medium size raw shrimp, shelled and
    deveined, cut in half lengthwise
½ pound bay scallops
20 Ritz crackers, crushed
1 cup seasoned breadcrumbs

Juice from one lemon
¼ teaspoon black pepper
¼ teaspoon garlic powder
2 cups fresh baby spinach leaves
1 can Campbell's Cream of Shrimp soup
¾ cup sour cream
½ cup white wine
1 teaspoon paprika
¼ cup fresh parsley, chopped

Preheat over to 375 degrees.

Place each chicken breast in a Ziploc™ bag and pound with a mallet to flatten to even ½-inch thickness all over. Set aside.

Melt butter in a large skillet. Sauté onion and celery until soft, about 3-4 minutes. Add shrimp and scallops and cook until just barely cooked through, 2 minutes. Remove from heat and add crackers, breadcrumbs, lemon juice, pepper and garlic powder to pan and mix until well combined. Let stuffing cool completely (this can be done a day in advance).

Lay the pounded chicken breasts out on a large cutting board and liberally salt and pepper both sides.

Divide the stuffing into 8 parts. Place ¼ cup of the spinach leaves on each breast. Place a mound of stuffing in the middle of each breast and roll jellyroll style. Place each breast, seam side down, in a greased 9x13-inch baking dish.

In a small bowl whisk together the Campbell's soup, sour cream, wine, and parsley. Pour evenly over the chicken breasts. Sprinkle with paprika.

Bake for 45 minutes to 1 hour or until chicken is just cooked through. Remove from oven, garnish with parsley, and serve over rice pilaf with peas on the side. Delicious!!!

Serves 8

Rate It!
☆☆☆☆☆

chicken and sun-dried tomato cream sauce
over linguini

1, 8.5 ounce jar sun-dried tomatoes (packed in oil), coarsely chopped or julienned
1 large onion, chopped
6 cloves garlic, chopped
1 pint mushrooms, sliced
½ cup dry white wine
4 cups boneless chicken breast, cooked and shredded into bite-size pieces (about 3 boneless breasts)
1 teaspoon salt
1 teaspoon black pepper
1 tablespoon dried basil
1 heaping tablespoon corn starch
1 cup milk
1 cup heavy cream
1 cup parmesan cheese, plus more on the side for sprinkling
1 pound linguini pasta, cooked al dente
½ cup fresh basil, leaves chiffonade (or chopped), plus more for garnish

Drain the oil from the jar of sun-dried tomatoes into a large deep skillet and sauté onions and garlic over medium heat until soft and fragrant. Add the mushrooms and cook, stirring frequently, about 3-4 minutes. Add the wine to the pan and simmer until about half of the liquid has cooked off, another 2-3 minutes.

Add the sun-dried tomatoes, chicken, salt, pepper, and basil to the pan and mix to combine. Whisk the corn starch with the milk in a small bowl. Pour into the pan and add heavy cream. Cook for 2-3 minutes, stirring frequently until the sauce comes to a low boil and begins to thicken. Gradually stir in the parmesan cheese and cook for 1-2 minutes until sauce is rich and thick. Toss the fresh basil and pasta in the sauce until coated.

Serve hot in bowls and sprinkle with parmesan cheese and more fresh chopped basil to garnish.

Serves 6-8

Rate It!
☆☆☆☆☆

greek chicken casserole

½ cup olive oil
¼ cup red wine vinegar
¼ cup orange juice
2 tablespoons lemon juice
1 teaspoon Dijon mustard
3 teaspoons **Dish off the Block Ciao Bella Italian Spice Blend**
½ teaspoon salt
1 teaspoon black pepper
3 garlic cloves, chopped
3-3.5 pounds boneless, skinless, chicken thighs and/or breasts

1, 6.9 ounce box Near East rice pilaf mix
2, 10 ounce boxes frozen chopped spinach, thawed
½ cup chicken stock
1 pint grape or cherry tomatoes, cut into quarters or 3 large tomatoes, rough chopped (about 2 cups)
8 ounces feta cheese,
1, 2.25 ounce can sliced black olives (or ½ cup Kalamata olives, chopped)
2 tablespoons fresh parsley, chopped

Preheat oven to 375 degrees.

Combine olive oil, vinegar, orange juice, lemon juice, Dijon, Italian seasoning, salt, pepper, and chopped garlic in a large jar and shake vigorously to combine and emulsify.

Put the chicken thighs in a large Ziploc™ bag with the dressing and massage to ensure the chicken is well coated all over. Marinate for at least 1 hour or as long as overnight (the longah, the bettah!).

In a 9x13-inch pan, sprinkle the rice pilaf contents, including spice packet, evenly over the bottom of the pan. Then, top evenly with the thawed spinach, including spinach juices. Pour chicken stock over the spinach.

Lay chicken pieces on top of spinach, including marinade.

Spread tomatoes over chicken, followed by crumbled feta cheese. Cover with foil and bake for 40 minutes.

Remove from oven and sprinkle evenly with the olives. Return to oven for 25-30 minutes until chicken is cooked through and cheese is lightly browned. Garnish with parsley and serve.

Serves 6-8

Rate It!
☆☆☆☆☆

honey mustard chicken

1 cup honey
½ cup Dijon mustard
½ cup whole grain mustard
3 tablespoons fresh ginger root, chopped
2 teaspoons salt
2 teaspoons black pepper

6 boneless chicken breasts, pounded to
    ½-inch thickness
¼ cup vegetable oil
4 tablespoons butter
2 cups pecans, finely chopped
2 cups panko breadcrumbs

Whisk honey, mustards and ginger together in a small bowl. Season chicken breasts on both sides with salt and pepper. Spread 1 tablespoon of honey mustard sauce on each side of chicken to coat and place in a 9x13-inch pan to marinate for at least 2 hours or overnight. Reserve remaining sauce.

Preheat oven to 350 degrees.

Heat oil in a large skillet over medium heat. Mix pecans and bread crumbs in a shallow baking dish. Press each honey-mustard-coated breast into the breadcrumb/pecan coating to fully coat. Place in hot oil and brown on each side, flipping gingerly to make sure crust adheres. Repeat for each breast, adding oil to the pan as needed.

Place browned breasts back into the 9x13-inch pan (on top of any remaining marinade). Bake until chicken is just cooked through, about 10-15 minutes depending on the size of the breasts. Heat remaining sauce in a small saucepan and drizzle over the cooked chicken.*

*I also like to make carrots with this dish (peel, slice, and boil until fork tender) and also top or toss with the remaining honey mustard sauce.

Serves 6-8

Rate It!
☆☆☆☆☆

honey mustard chicken thighs
with apples and onions

2 tablespoons olive oil
6 chicken thighs, bone-in and skin on
2 teaspoons salt
2 teaspoons black pepper
2 large onions, sliced into 1-inch wedges
3 apples, sliced into 1-inch wedges (any good 'cooking' apples such as Granny Smith, Pink Lady, Cortland, Honey Crisp, etc...)

10 sprigs of thyme, tied together with kitchen string
1 cup white wine
¾ cup honey
½ cup Dijon
¼ cup grainy mustard

Preheat oven to 400 degrees.

Heat olive oil in a large cast iron or oven proof skillet over medium high heat.

Trim any excess fat off the chicken thighs and season liberally on both sides with 1 teaspoon each of the salt and pepper. Place the seasoned thighs, skin-side down in the skillet and let cook until the skin is browned and crispy, about 4-5 minutes. Flip and cook for 2 minutes on the other side. Remove from pan and set aside, reserving pan drippings. Note—the chicken will not be cooked through.

Add the onions to the skillet and cook, stirring frequently, until they begin to get soft. Add the apples and thyme bundle to the pan and cook for 2 more minutes, still stirring. Add the wine to the pan and deglaze, scraping up all of the brown bits on the bottom of the pan. Season with remaining salt and pepper. Cook for 3 minutes, letting the wine reduce.

While this cooks, combine the honey with both mustards in a small bowl and whisk until smooth.

Place the chicken thighs back in the pan, nestled in the onions and apples, skin side up. Pour the honey mustard sauce evenly over the thighs. Bake for 30 minutes until chicken is cooked through and a luxurious sauce has formed. Discard the thyme bundle to the trash. Serve over rice pilaf or quinoa to absorb the delicious sauce. Garnish with thyme sprigs and DEVOUR!

Serves 6

Rate It!
☆☆☆☆☆

thai-riffic! chicken and shrimp naan pizza

This pizza won the 2019 Taste of America Contest and a Golden ticket to the World Food Championships!

THE SAUCE:

2 large cloves garlic, peeled and minced
2 teaspoons fresh ginger, minced
1 teaspoon red pepper flakes
3 tablespoons light brown sugar, packed
⅓ cup creamy peanut butter

3 tablespoons soy sauce
1 tablespoon fish sauce
1 cup boneless chicken breasts, cooked and
    shredded into bite-size pieces

THE SHRIMP AND PEA PODS:

2 tablespoons butter
12 ounces large raw Shrimp, peeled and deveined (about 10 large shrimps)
¾ cup pea pods

THE PIZZA:

1, 8.8 oz. package Naan flatbreads (2, 10-12-
    inch flatbreads)
⅓ cup canned water chestnuts, drained and
    rough chopped
1 small jalapeno, sliced thin into rounds
⅓ cup red bell pepper, chopped

⅓ cup fresh bean sprouts
½ cup shredded Monterey Jack cheese
2 scallions, chopped
1 heaping tablespoon cilantro, chopped
1 heaping tablespoon basil, chiffonade
2 tablespoons honey roasted peanuts, chopped

Preheat oven to 425 degrees and set rack to the lowest position in your oven.

In a small bowl, whisk together the garlic, ginger, red pepper flakes, brown sugar, peanut butter, soy sauce, and fish sauce until smooth in consistency. Add the chicken to the sauce and toss to coat. Set aside.

Melt the butter in a large skillet over medium high heat. When the pan is very hot, add the shrimp and the pea pods and spread into one layer. Let cook one minute until shrimp begin to turn pink. Toss with tongs until shrimp are just cooked through and the pea pods are crisp tender, about another minute.

Place the naan flatbreads on a foil-lined baking sheet. Spread chicken and sauce mixture evenly over the naan breads leaving a little of the crust/edge area exposed. Continue evenly layering the water chestnuts, jalapeno, red bell pepper, shrimp, pea pods, bean sprouts, and Monterey Jack cheese.

Bake for 10-12 minutes until the cheese is melted and the sauce is bubbly. Remove from oven and sprinkle with the scallions, cilantro, basil, and chopped peanuts.

Serves 2-4.

Rate It!
☆☆☆☆

lemon cream pasta
with chicken, mushrooms, & peas

4 tablespoons butter
1 leek, white and light green parts chopped
8 cloves garlic, peeled and chopped
8 ounces cremini mushrooms, sliced
1 tablespoon fresh thyme leaves, stemmed
½ cup dry white wine
½ cup chicken stock
2 cups heavy cream
2 teaspoons salt
2 teaspoons black pepper

2 lemons, zested and juiced (about 2 tablespoons zest and ¼ cup juice)
2 cups boneless chicken breast, cooked and shredded
1 cup parmesan cheese (plus more for sprinkling on finished dish)
2 cups frozen peas, thawed
1/3 cup flat leaf parsley, chopped (plus more for garnish)
1 pound spaghetti, cooked al dente according to package directions

Sauté the leeks and garlic in the butter over medium high heat in a large deep skillet until soft and fragrant, about 2 minutes. Add the mushrooms and thyme leaves to the pan and continue to cook, stirring frequently until the mushrooms have released their moisture and started to lightly brown.

Add the wine and chicken stock to the pan and let cook for 4-5 minutes at a low boil until it has reduced by about ⅓. Add the heavy cream, salt, and pepper to the pan and cook for another 5 minutes letting the sauce further reduce and thicken.

Stir in the lemon zest, lemon juice, and chicken. Gradually add the parmesan cheese, stirring constantly at a low boil. Cook for 2 minutes and remove from heat. Add the peas, parsley, and spaghetti to the sauce and toss until well coated.

Serve in large bowls and garnish with additional parmesan, chopped parsley, and lemon slices.

Serves 6-8

Rate It!

italian chicken skillet bake

THE CHICKEN:

2.5-3 pounds boneless chicken breasts
1 teaspoon salt
1 teaspoon black pepper
¼-½ cup olive oil
½ cup Hellmann's Light mayonnaise

2 tablespoons **Dish off the Block Ciao Bella Italian Spice Blend**
¾ cup grated parmesan cheese
¾ cup panko bread crumbs
¼ cup olive oil

THE SAUCE:

1 large onion, chopped
1 small green pepper, chopped
1 small red bell pepper, chopped
2 small zucchinis, chopped into ½-inch thick crescents
½ cup dry red wine
1, 28 ounce can San Marzano tomatoes

1 tablespoon brown sugar
1 teaspoon salt
1 teaspoon black pepper
3 teaspoons **Dish off the Block Ciao Bella Italian Spice Blend**

THE CHEESE AND GARNISH:

1 cup mozzarella
½ cup fresh basil, chiffonade
¼ cup flat leaf parsley, chopped

1 pound orzo pasta, cooked according to package directions

Preheat oven to 375 degrees and heat ¼ cup of the olive oil in a large deep oven-proof skillet. (If you do not have an oven proof skillet, you can make the dish in a non-stick skillet and transfer to a baking dish.)

Season the chicken breasts with the salt and pepper on both sides. If they are very large, cut into portion size pieces. Otherwise, they can remain whole.

Combine the mayonnaise with **Italian Spice Blend** in a small bowl and combine the parmesan and panko in a pie plate or shallow baking dish.

Using a pastry brush, coat the chicken breasts with the herby mayo and then press into the parmesan bread crumbs on both sides (reserve any remaining crumbs). Place in the hot oil and cook about 2 minutes per side until golden brown. Gingerly flip after the first side is browned so that the crumbs adhere to the chicken. You may need to work in batches and add more olive oil as needed.

Note—chicken will not be cooked through. Set aside.

Rate It!
☆☆☆☆☆

To the same pan, add more olive oil as needed to coat the bottom of the pan. Add onion, green and red peppers to the skillet and cook until soft and fragrant, about 3 minutes. Add the zucchini and cook another 3 minutes until tender and the veggies start to lightly caramelize.

Add the red wine, tomatoes, brown sugar, salt, pepper, and **Italian Spice Blend** to the pan. Bring to a boil and crush the tomatoes with your spatula. Snuggle the chicken into the sauce leaving the tops exposed. Sprinkle with any remaining parmesan crumbs and place in the oven. Bake for 15 minutes.

Remove from oven and top with the mozzarella cheese. Place back in the oven for 15-20 minutes until cheese is melted and lightly browned—and chicken is cooked through. Remove and let rest for 10 minutes. Serve over orzo, garnished with fresh basil and parsley.

Serves 6-8

chicken, winter squash, bacon, and arugula parmesan gratin casserole

½ pound bacon slices
2 large leeks, cleaned and chopped (about 3 cups)
4 large garlic cloves, peeled and chopped
3 pounds winter squash, cut into 1-inch cubes, about 4-5 cups (peeled butternut or acorn, delicata, kombucha, etc...)
3 cups baby arugula, baby kale, or baby spinach leaves (or combo), packed

2 ½ cups cooked and shredded chicken breast (leftover chicken or turkey great for this!)
1 teaspoon salt
1 teaspoon black pepper
1 cup grated parmesan cheese
1 pint heavy cream
¾ cup panko bread crumbs
1 tablespoon olive oil
2 tablespoons flat leaf parsley, chopped for garnish

Preheat oven to 375 degrees.

Cook bacon in a large skillet over medium high heat until just crisp. Remove from pan and let drain on paper towels, then chop into ½-inch pieces. Add the leeks to the remaining bacon grease and sauté until tender and fragrant, about 5 minutes

Coat a 9x13-inch baking dish with non-stick cooking spray. Combine the squash, arugula, and chicken in the baking dish and toss to evenly distribute. Season with the salt and pepper.

Top with the squash evenly with the sautéed leeks, followed by bacon, parmesan, and finally pour the cream over the casserole, using a fork to gently 'move' the contents so the cream can flow into the nooks and crannies.

Combine the panko and olive oil in a small bowl. Sprinkle over the top of the casserole.

Cover with foil and bake for 30 minutes. Remove foil and bake for an additional 30-40 minutes until bubbly, browned, and the squash is very tender throughout when pierced with a fork. Garnish with parsley and serve hot.

Serves 6-8

Rate It!

spaghetti squash and chicken burrito bowls

THE SQUASH:

1 spaghetti squash
2 tablespoons olive oil

1 teaspoon salt
½ teaspoon black pepper

THE CHICKEN:

1 tablespoon olive oil
2 boneless, skinless chicken breasts (about 1 pound)

3 teaspoons **Dish off the Block Ragin' Cajun Spice Blend**
¼ teaspoon cumin

THE FILLING:

1 medium onion, chopped
1 small green bell pepper, chopped
1 jalapeno, chopped including seeds
1 small red bell pepper, chopped
1 cup frozen corn, thawed

1, 10.5 ounce can black beans, drained and rinsed
1 cup salsa (your favorite brand)
2 ¾ cups grated sharp cheddar cheese
½ cup tomatoes, chopped

THE GARNISH:

¼ cup cilantro leaves, chopped
½ cup sour cream
2 limes, cut into wedges

Preheat oven to 375 degrees.

Cut the spaghetti squash in half lengthwise and scoop out the seeds in the center with a spoon and discard. Drizzle 2 tablespoons of the olive oil over the cut side of the squash and sprinkle with 1 teaspoon each of the salt and pepper. Place cut-side down on a foil-lined baking sheet. Bake for 45 minutes to 1 hour until very tender when pierced with a fork. Let cool for 10-15 minutes until you can handle with your hands. When cool enough to handle, shred the squash with a fork and set aside, leaving the shells intact.

While the squash cooks. Heat the olive oil in a large deep skillet. Cut the chicken breast into 2-3-inch cubes. Sprinkle the **Dish off the Block Ragin' Cajun Spice Blend** over the chicken and rub it in to coat on all sides. Add the seasoned chicken to the hot oil and cook about 2 minutes per side until just cooked through. Remove the chicken from the pan, reserving the drippings and set aside.

Rate It!
☆☆☆☆

Add the onion, green bell pepper, and jalapeno to the pan and sauté until soft and fragrant. Add the red bell pepper to the pan and cook for 2 more minutes. Remove from heat and add the shredded squash to the pan along with the corn, beans, salsa, and chicken. Stir to combine. Add 2 cups of the shredded cheddar cheese to the pan and mix well.

Scoop the squash mixture back into the squash shells and top with the chopped tomatoes and remaining cheese. Place back in the oven and bake for 15-20 minutes until the cheese is melted and bubbly.

Garnish with cilantro and serve with sour cream and lime wedges on the side.

Serves 4-6

coconut crusted chicken
with spicy pineapple sauce

THE CHICKEN:

4-6, boneless, skinless, chicken breast halves, about
   3 pounds
2 teaspoons salt
1 teaspoon black pepper

2 cups flaked coconut
1 cup panko bread crumbs
3 eggs
½ cup vegetable oil

THE SAUCE:

1, 20 ounce can pineapple chunks in syrup
¾ cup apricot preserves
1 jalapeño, rough chopped including seeds
½ cup sweetened coconut flakes
1, 13.7 oz. can coconut milk
1 teaspoon salt

THE PINEAPPLE AND RICE:

2 tablespoons. butter
1, 20 oz. can pineapple chunks, drained
3 cups cooked jasmine rice, cooked to package
   directions
¼ cup fresh cilantro, chopped

Preheat oven to 350 degrees.

Pound chicken breasts with a mallet to ½-inch thickness. Season on both sides with salt and pepper.

In one shallow dish, combine the coconut flakes and panko crumbs. In another shallow dish, beat the eggs.

Heat the oil in a large skillet over medium high heat.

Coat the chicken breasts into the egg first and then the coconut crumb mixture pressing to adhere. Add the chicken to the pan in one layer, in batches if necessary. Cook for 2-3 minutes per side until coconut is golden brown. Transfer the cooked breasts to a cookie sheet and bake in the oven while you make the sauce for 15-20 minutes until the chicken is just cooked through.

Combine pineapple in syrup, apricot preserves, jalapeno, flaked coconut, coconut milk, and salt in a blender and blend until smooth. Place in a sauce pan over medium heat and cook for 3-5 minutes stirring frequently until hot and bubbly.

Melt the butter in a large frying pan over medium high heat. Add drained pineapple chunks and cook until pineapple is lightly browned and caramelized, about 3 minutes, stirring occasionally.

Serve one chicken breast over rice topped with sauce and garnished with pineapple chunks and cilantro.

Serves 6-8

Rate It!

☆☆☆☆☆

chicken and mussels in fennel tarragon cream sauce
over sticky rice

I love pairing chicken with seafood and we are lucky to have access to fresh local mussels in the summer on Block Island. I created this dish after a bountiful day of harvesting mussels with my son, Andrew. Notes of anise from fennel and tarragon elevate the flavor profile of the cream sauce to new heights and really complement the sweet mussels and tender chicken.

1 ½ cups sushi rice, raw
3 tablespoons olive oil
2 leeks, chopped (white and light
    green parts)
1 fennel bulb, chopped
6 large garlic cloves, chopped
3 large chicken breasts, sliced on
    the bias into bite size pieces
    (about 3 cups)
2 teaspoons salt
2 teaspoons black pepper
¼ cup Sambuca or Pernod liqueur

⅓ cup dry white wine
2 cups heavy cream
3 tablespoons fresh tarragon,
    chopped
3 tablespoons fresh basil, chopped
½ teaspoon red pepper flakes
2 tablespoons soy sauce
3 pounds fresh mussels, in shells,
    beards removed

Combine sushi rice with 2 cups of water in a medium size sauce pan. Bring to a boil, cover and reduce to simmer until all liquid is absorbed.

Add olive oil to a large skillet with sides, over medium high heat. Add leeks, fennel, and garlic to the pan. Stir occasionally until the veggies begin to get soft and translucent, about 5 minutes.

Add chicken to the pan and stir to combine. Add salt and pepper and let cook until chicken begins to cook through. Add Sambuca, wine, and cream to the pan and let boil lightly over medium high heat for about 10 minutes until sauce begins to reduce and chicken is cooked through.

Add tarragon, basil, red pepper flakes, soy sauce, and mussels to the pan. Cover and cook for another 5-7 minutes until the mussels open.

Serve over the sticky rice... Delish!!

Serves 6-8

Rate It!
☆☆☆☆☆

chicken primavera fettucini alfredo

4 large carrots, sliced in ¼-inch slices
4 cups broccoli florets
1 cup pea pods
5 tablespoons butter
1 small onion, chopped
6 cloves garlic, chopped
1 red bell pepper, cut into slices and chopped to
    2-inch pieces
1 small zucchini, cut into ¼-inch half moons
½ cup white wine
2 pints heavy cream or whipping cream
4 ounces cream cheese, softened
2 cups grated parmesan cheese
3 cups cooked shredded chicken
    (bite size pieces)
1 pound fettuccini pasta, cooked al dente to package directions
2 tablespoons fresh basil leaves, chiffonade

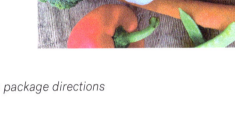

Boil a large pot of water with 1 tablespoon salt. Add carrots and let boil until barely fork tender. Add broccoli and boil for 10 minutes more until broccoli is just tender. Add pea pods and boil for one minute longer. Drain and rinse with cold water to stop cooking.

Melt butter in large deep skillet. Add onion and garlic and sauté until soft and fragrant over medium heat. Add red bell pepper and zucchini, and continue to sauté until tender. Add white wine and let reduce, about 3 minutes. Add cream and cream cheese and whisk constantly until smooth and creamy. Let simmer and reduce for 5 minutes. Whisk in parmesan. Add broccoli, carrots, pea pods, chicken, and pasta. Toss to combine and fully coat the pasta.

Serve garnished with basil and extra parmesan on the side. Put on your spandex pants and dig in!

Serves 4-6

Rate It!
☆☆☆☆☆

chicken milanese
with arugula salad and lemon cream sauce

THE SAUCE:

6 tablespoons butter
6 large garlic cloves, chopped
2 teaspoons flour
¼ cup white wine

3 cups heavy cream
1 teaspoon salt
zest from 2 lemons
juice from 2 lemons

THE CHICKEN:

3-3 ½ pounds boneless chicken breast
2-3 teaspoons salt
2-3 teaspoons black pepper
1 cup flour
3 eggs

1 ½ cups Italian seasoned breadcrumbs
1 cup panko breadcrumbs
¾ cup grated parmesan cheese
¾ cup chopped flat leaf parsley
½ cup olive oil

THE SALAD:

3 cups baby arugula leaves
½ cup shaved parmesan flakes

1 tablespoons olive oil
2 tablespoons lemon juice

THE PASTA:

1 pound angel hair pasta, cooked al dente to package directions

Make the sauce. In a large saucepan, melt the butter over medium heat. Add the garlic and sauté until soft and fragrant, about 1 minute. Add flour and stir to combine and cook for one more minute. Add the wine, heavy cream, salt, and lemon zest. Bring to a low boil and reduce the heat to medium low and let boil lightly while you prepare the chicken, stirring frequently. Sauce should reduce by a third. Just before serving, stir in the lemon juice and cook for 2 more minutes.

Place each chicken breast on a cutting board and put one hand on top of the breast. With the other hand, carefully slice the breast in half horizontally (butterfly), creating 2 thin cutlets. Place each cutlet in a large Ziploc™ bag (or between sheets of wax paper) and pound to ¼-inch thickness all over with a meat pounder. Liberally season the chicken cutlets on both sides with salt and pepper.

Create a dredging station with 3 shallow baking dishes or pie plates. Put the flour in the first dish. Scramble the eggs in the second dish. Combine the Italian breadcrumbs, panko, parmesan, and parsley in the third dish and mix well to combine.

Take each cutlet and first dredge in the flour, shaking off excess. Then, dip in the egg, letting excess run off and press into the breadcrumb mixture to fully coat.

Rate It!
☆☆☆☆

Heat half of the olive oil over medium high heat in a large skillet. Working in batches, careful not to crowd the chicken, place each cutlet in the oil and cook to golden brown on each side, about 2 minutes per side. Add more oil as needed.

To make the salad, toss arugula with shaved parmesan, olive oil and lemon juice. Salt and pepper to taste.

Serve one cutlet drizzled with lemon cream sauce and topped with arugula salad. Place one serving of angel hair on the side topped with more of the lemon cream sauce.

You can also serve this dish without the pasta and cut the cream sauce recipe in half which is tradition-al... but dang the pasta with the lemon cream is deeeeelisshhhh!

Serves 6-8

chicken divan

3-4 cups broccoli florets
1 ½ pounds raw boneless chicken breast, chopped into 2-inch pieces (about 3 cups)
2 teaspoons **Dish off the Block Superbly Herby Spice Blend**
1 teaspoon salt
1 teaspoon black pepper
6 tablespoons butter, divided

1 medium onion, chopped
½ cup dry white wine
½ cup chicken stock
1 cup light cream
½ cup sour cream
2 cups shredded cheddar cheese
1 cup raw rice, cooked to package directions (about 2 ½ cups cooked rice)
40 Ritz crackers, crushed in a Ziploc™ bag

Preheat oven to 375 degrees.

Bring a large sauce pan of salted water to a boil and add the broccoli. Cook for 3-4 minutes until the broccoli is bright green and tender when pierced with a fork, but still slightly crisp. Drain in a colander and run cold water over it to stop the cooking. Set aside.

Place the chicken breast cubes on a cutting board and sprinkle the **Superbly Herby Spice Blend**, salt, and pepper over the top. Massage the seasoning all over the chicken with your hands.

Melt 4 tablespoons of the butter in a large deep skillet. Add the chicken and cook for 2-3 minutes, lightly browning on all sides. Remove from the skillet and set aside—note: the chicken will not be cooked through.

To the drippings in the pan, add the onion and cook until soft and fragrant, about 2 minutes. Add the wine to the pan and cook until reduced by half. Add the cream and sour cream and bring to a boil, stirring frequently. Cook for 2-3 minutes until a cream sauce forms.

Add the cheese and stir until melted. Fold in the rice, chicken pieces (and any juices that have formed), and broccoli. Transfer this mixture to a 9x13-inch pan that has been prepared with non-stick spray.

Melt the remaining 2 tablespoons butter in the empty skillet and add the crushed Ritz cracker crumbs. Cook until lightly browned and spread them evenly over the top of the casserole.

Bake for 25-30 minutes until bubbly and browned.

Serves 6-8

Rate It!
☆☆☆☆☆

chicken, pineapple, and pepper teriyaki stir fry boats

THE CHICKEN:

1 ½ pounds boneless chicken breasts
1 teaspoon salt
1 tablespoon peanut or vegetable oil
1 tablespoon rice wine vinegar

1 tablespoon soy sauce
1 egg white, beaten until frothy
2 tablespoons corn starch

THE STIR FRY:

6 tablespoons peanut or vegetable oil
1 fresh pineapple (or 1, 20 ounce can
     pineapple chunks in juice)
1 large onion, chopped
8 garlic cloves, chopped
1 jalapeno, chopped (including seeds)
1 tablespoon fresh ginger root, minced
1 green pepper, chopped into 1-inch pieces
1 red bell pepper, chopped into 1-inch pieces

¼ cup soy sauce
¼ cup pineapple juice (or orange juice)
½ cup chicken stock
1 teaspoon sesame oil
½ cup brown sugar
2 tablespoons hoisin sauce
½ teaspoon black pepper
1 tablespoon corn starch

3 cups cooked sushi rice (about 1 ½ cups raw rice)
¼ cup scallions, chopped

Slice the chicken breasts into ½-inch thick slices across the grain and place in a small bowl. If they are large, you may want to cut them in half lengthwise first, so you end up with bite-size pieces. Also, if you partially freeze the breasts before cutting, they are easier to handle and slice thin.

Add the salt, oil, vinegar, soy sauce, egg white, and corn starch to the bowl and toss everything together until the chicken is well coated. Let marinate for 30 minutes while you prepare the pineapple and vegetables for the stir fry.

If you are using a fresh whole pineapple, cut it in half lengthwise and then, using a paring knife, cut around the inside of the shell and scoop out the flesh leaving the 'shells' intact to use as your serving dishes. Cut the hard core from the center of the pineapple and chop the remaining pineapple flesh into bite size chunks. Be sure to reserve any juice that forms.

If you are using canned pineapple, simply drain the chunks and reserve the juice for the sauce.

Heat 5 tablespoons of the peanut oil in a large skillet (or wok if you have one) over medium high heat. When the oil is very hot, add the marinated chicken to the pan and cook, tossing constantly

Rate It!
☆☆☆☆

with a spatula until the chicken is just barely opaque. It will continue to cook later in the sauce so it does not need to be cooked through, just seared. Remove from pan and set aside.

Add the additional 1 tablespoon of oil to the pan drippings and add the onions, garlic, jalapeno, and ginger root. Cook, stirring frequently, and scraping up any brown bits from the bottom of the pan until fragrant, about 2 minutes. Add the green and red bell peppers and pineapple to the pan. Cook over medium high heat for 4-5 minutes until peppers are soft and the pineapple begins to get golden brown caramelization. Add the chicken back to the pan with any juices.

Whisk the soy sauce, pineapple (or orange) juice, chicken stock, sesame oil, brown sugar, hoisin, black pepper, and corn starch in a small bowl until smooth. Add the sauce to the pan and cook, stirring constantly, until everything is coated and a thick glossy sauce forms, about 2 minutes.

If serving in the pineapple shells, line each shell with the rice and fill with the stir fry mixture. Garnish with scallions. Otherwise, get yourself a big ole bowl and fill 'er up!!

Serves 4-6

Bon appétit!

Hope you enjoyed
your frickin' chicken ...

Find hundreds more recipes on the blog at
dishofftheblock.com and share pictures of your
DotB creations on social media using the hashtag
#dishofftheblock.

 dishofftheblock

 dishblock

 dishofftheblock

Pamela Gelsomini is a self-taught cook and consummate foodie who has spent decades traveling the globe in search of flavors that inspire creative cuisine. In 2017, following the sale of the footwear component company she co-founded, Pam took her infatuation with food to the next level, launching a new career as a lifestyle blogger and award-winning food sport competitor. Pam, a wife and mother, has reinvented herself in her second act and urges others to tap into their own artistry in order to try something new. That may start with a simple yet sophisticated meal! Find hundreds of Pam's unique—yet easy-to-make—recipes on her blog: dishofftheblock.com.

CPSIA information can be obtained
at www.ICGtesting.com
Printed in the USA
JSHW041124261120
9841JS00002B/2